WOMEN'S LEADERSHIP IN A CHANGING WORLD

Reflecting on Experience in Latin America and the Caribbean

Edited by ANA MARIA BRASILEIRO

UNIFEM

United Nations Development Fund for Women (UNIFEM)
New York, USA

The United Nations Development Fund for Women (UNIFEM) was created as a result of the energetic advocacy of women at the 1975 International Women's Year (IWY) Tribune in Mexico City. Established by the United Nations in 1976 as the Voluntary Fund for the UN Decade for Women, UNIFEM became an autonomous organization within the UN family in 1985. UNIFEM provides direct technical and financial support to programmes that promote women. By supporting the full participation of women in the developing world to achieve their objectives of political and economic empowerment. UNIFEM works to improve the quality of life for all. This collection of articles is the second of a four-part series that reflects on UNIFEM's experience with projects and programmes in Latin America and the Caribbean.

Women's Leadership in a Changing World
Edited by Ana Maria Brasileiro
ISBN 0-912917-40-7
Series Title: Reflecting on Experience

United Nations Development Fund for Women
304 East 45th Street, 6th Floor, New York, NY 10017 USA
Phone: (212) 906-6400 Fax: (212) 906-6705

All UNIFEM publications are distributed by Women, Ink.
777 UN Plaza, 3rd Floor, New York, NY 10017 USA
Phone: (212) 687-8633 Fax: (212) 661-2704

SPONSORED BY THE GOVERNMENT OF JAPAN

Cover & book design by a. piccolo graphics

Table of Contents

We dedicate this book to Dame Nita Barrow

In a life's work that spanned most of the twentieth century, Dame Nita Barrow taught us about the essential leadership qualities that make transformation and empowerment possible. The leading role that she played in so many countries and institutions—whether as a student nurse in Barbados, as the first black president of the World YWCA in Geneva, as her country's Permanent Representative to the United Nations headquarters in New York, or as the remarkable convenor of the Third UN World Conference on Women in Nairobi in 1985—was marked by commitment, compassion, humour, vision and a sense of responsibility to those who would follow her. Dame Nita embodied the ideal of the enlightened leader.

Acknowledgements

This book represents much more than the thinking and writing of the women whose names are listed as contributors. It is a reflection of two decades of work by thousands of women in Latin America and the Caribbean who have refused to be silent in the face of the increasing inability of states to meet the basic needs of citizens. These women, too numerous to name, have built valuable leadership skills and have struggled to exercise them in the public arena. Working in grassroots communities or feminist organizations, in offices, small businesses, or non-profit organizations, they have demonstrated a new capacity and new style of leadership. It is because of them that a collection such as this one is now possible.

The voices and experiences of women activists, advocates and academics in countries and communities worldwide come to us at the UNIFEM headquarters in New York through our network of Regional Programme Advisors (RPAs). The articles in this book and the inspiration for pulling them together could not have come about without in-depth consultation with Guadalupe Espinosa in Mexico, Joycelin Massiah in Barbados, Branca Moreira Alves in Brazil, and Monica Muñoz in Ecuador. Guadalupe Espinosa in our Mexico office and Karen Judd and Joanne Sandler at headquarters took responsibility for editing the manuscripts and moving the production process along. Claudine Correia, Programme Officer in the Latin American/Caribbean section at UNIFEM, and Ana Cecilia Quintanilla, who has backstopped so many efforts for this section, were also valuable and committed partners in this effort.

Finally, we need to acknowledge our colleagues at UNIFEM, who are tireless in their efforts to advocate and raise funds for women's efforts worldwide. It is the collective effort of all UNIFEM staff that keeps the UN support for women's organizing and empowerment alive. ❖

—Ana Maria Brasileiro

"Old styles of leadership cannot adequately address our new world situation or new world problems. We need a style of leadership that does not exercise power over people, resources and territories but instead exercises power with *them. This leadership should not dominate or coerce but rather facilitate and empower. It should lead by allowing people to grow."*

"... Women now have a leading role to play, not only in building a new vision of development, but in the implementation of systems and processes that will create a sustainable future for all."

—Noeleen Heyzer, Introduction,
Commitment to the World's Women, UNIFEM, 1995

Preface

SHARON CAPELING-ALAKIJA

The United Nations has made a tremendous investment in women, providing a platform from which women can mobilize resources, articulate and refine issues, and plan strategy. It has provided opportunities for the women of the world to come together, to be energized, to move forward and to learn from each other, to begin to understand the nature of the humanity we share as women and to begin to acknowledge and negotiate the profound differences among us.

Like many women working in international agencies, I'm cognizant of the contradictions involved in this work. I am acutely aware of the fact that we are trying to create change for women with instruments and institutions designed by and for men. My colleagues and I have long wrestled with the warning of the poet Audre Lorde that "the Master's tools will never dismantle the Master's house."

After all, women have always been left out of institutions of governance. We see them with the outsider's eye—even those of us who have become insiders. In a short time, we have learned how to participate effectively in the international arena. Over the past 20 years, we have learned the logistics necessary for effective participation in UN World Conferences—how to get accredited, how to work a UN preparatory committee meeting, how to pass this know-how on to other women. We have learned to use telecommunications to reinforce and expand our networks.

Far more important than the conferences themselves is the work that goes on before and after meetings—the researching, documenting, petitioning, drafting, lobbying, legislating. Twenty years of those exercises, from Mexico City to Copenhagen to Nairobi and beyond, have altered our notions of what it means to be a woman in the twentieth century.

Occasionally it occurs to me that those of us who devote our lives to the international women's movement may seem like profoundly gray, bureaucratic figures as we debate procedural points and agenda planks. The process is evolutionary, not revolutionary. We're not at the barricades; we're at the table. And most of the time, it's not even our own table. When we make changes they are small, incremental. But because we are talking about the majority of the human race, very small changes can mean vastly improved conditions—even survival—for great numbers of women. If we turn the lens of the kaleidoscope just a few degrees, the realignment of shape and colour can create a very different pattern.

What is important here is that as women engage in the exercise of global governance, we are beginning to move towards a profoundly different way of managing the global commons. The substance of women's deliberations reflect a sense of the interconnectedness of issues, of the interdependency of North and South, of the possibilities and limitations of global governance.

From time to time, we humans appear to arrive at watershed moments—when practices once widely accepted become, if not repugnant to most people, at least unseemly. After all, in the last century we reached a point where the ownership of one human by another was deemed intolerable. As we edge towards a new century, I would like to hope that we will arrive at a moment when the exploitation and subjugation of women will be widely rejected.

I have little hope that in the next century we will wipe out discrimination against women altogether. But I do believe that together we will construct a human rights framework, a legal framework, a legislative framework, that will make bias and violence against women increasingly unacceptable. I do believe there will come a time when millions of women will no longer lose their lives, their freedom, or the possibility of fulfillment—simply because they are women. ❖

Introduction:
Can Women Change the World?

ANA MARIA BRASILEIRO AND KAREN JUDD

An integral part of the development of the women's movement everywhere is the recognition and growth of women's leadership, both within institutions and in society at large. The nature of this process in Latin America and the Caribbean, while not unique, is specific to the movements it has both grown out of and helped to propel. An examination of the experience of women's leadership at all levels sheds light on the creation and functioning of new spaces for women's participation, in both private and public institutions, as managers and executives, as entrepreneurs, in grassroots community organizing, in the creation and growth of women's organizations and in the new initiatives to make these organizations self-sustaining. In entering all of these arenas, many of them long dominated by men, women have assumed they would bring change, not only to the institutions but to the wider society, and in the process empower all women.

Women's efforts to bring about change did not occur in a vacuum. As a result of the globalization of markets for both capital and labour, the second half of the twentieth century witnessed drastic changes in the sexual division of labour throughout the region. Changes in family composition and dynamics, increased participation of women in the labour market and the entry of women onto the political scene have taken place alongside a process of urbanization and labour migration that increasingly leaves women in charge of the economic livelihood of the household. In Latin America as a whole, one in five families is now headed by a woman.

At the same time, some aspects of the division of labour have proven extremely resistant to change, notably the role of women in social reproduction. The expectation that women will continue to be the primary caregivers in the family and perform the unpaid labour in the household continues in countries throughout the world, an expectation that intensifies with increasing national debt, economic crisis and government austerity measures—conditions that have hit most of the countries in the region since the 1980s. In addition, the great fortresses of male power, the higher positions in government and, especially, in major private corporations, remain to a large extent closed to women. In Latin America, women occupy only 5 to 8 percent of legislative assembly positions and less than 6 percent of positions of authority in government. Moreover, women in government are overwhelmingly concentrated in "Women's Desks" and the social ministries, as they are in the Caribbean. The situation in business and industry is still worse, where only a tiny few occupy top corporate management positions.

Despite these barriers, however, women have come a long way in the struggle for the recognition of their rights. In Latin America, women have worked with policy makers and legislators to introduce changes in social and economic policy as well as in the laws and legal codes governing women's rights in these areas. Similarly in the Caribbean, while they have been less successful in shaping the direction of national development policy, women have managed, often with the support of those same Women's Desks, to change a number of laws governing their rights in such areas as marriage, divorce and custody, the status of children born out of wedlock, rape and sexual harassment, and equal pay and workplace discrimination.

The nature of women's achievements in large part reflects the development of their movements. In most of Latin America, for example, the women's movement grew and developed in tandem with the process of democratization in the region. However varied the democratization process, which, for example, took different paths in Central America than it did in countries of the Southern Cone, the cross-fertilization that resulted from this interaction gave to the women's movement an extraordinary dynamism and impact, confidence and credibility.

In the Caribbean, by contrast, the women's movement represents an evolving process that has gone through different phases that are linked by a common identification with basic survival needs. Most recently, it has taken shape in the context of a deepening economic crisis, which has challenged the credibility of governments and inherited democratic institutions. Feminist organizations, by organizing as part of community-based movements to design alternate development policies, have identified their interests with those of increasingly hard-pressed working-class and poor communities in many countries, and in so doing have sustained the vitality of their movement. In the Caribbean as in Latin America, therefore, the women's movement has been inspired in large part by the denial of participation, political or economic, to broad classes of people. As a result, the participation of grassroots women has been a crucial element in its vitality and legitimacy, enabling it to gain the broad-based support needed to effect meaningful social change.

Women's Paths to Power: Two Approaches

In Latin America and the Caribbean, as elsewhere, women have fought their battles from a number of positions, using different strategies and in many occasions aiming at different and seemingly contradictory targets. In looking at the history of women's efforts to bring about change, many observers have identified two basic ways in which women define their goals, derived from different conceptions of rights and responsibilities and resulting in different approaches to organizing for change. While the approaches have more in common than is sometimes acknowledged—indeed, their goals and strategies have frequently converged—it is nevertheless useful to distinguish between them, in part because their approaches are frequently associated with varied types of leadership and with the emergence or strengthening of different types of organizations.

The first approach is based on the identification of women with the role that society has allocated to them, especially that of caretakers. Women who take this approach, sometimes called "feminine," take very seriously the role assigned to them as mothers and caretakers, along with the expectations and valuation that goes with them. They react to situations that they perceive as threatening or unjust to those they are supposed to care for, or that prevent them from adequately carrying out their roles as caregivers in the family and community, by organizing to change these conditions.

One striking example of this approach is the Madres de la Plaza de Mayo in Argentina. The silent and persistent protest of Argentinian women in search of news of their children during the "dirty war" waged by the dictatorship against the people played a vital role in the redemocratization process in that country. But there are thousands of examples of women at the grassroots level organizing to demand services that will help them to fulfill their responsibilities—including water and sewerage provision, day care centres or health centres—or to protest policy decisions that make their lives as housewives or mothers more difficult. Especially in the Caribbean, as structural adjustment policies, including sharp cutbacks in social services, have imposed increased hardship on families, women have been expected to take on the tasks of providing for the basic needs of those who fell through the cracks, taking on both paid jobs in the labour force and unpaid caretaking activities in the home and community. Organizing in neighbourhood and community associations to deliver the services once provided by governments, women have developed leadership and negotiating skills. Some of them have become very influential in their respective communities, both internally and in their interaction with the outside world.

Although in many cases these movements are not comprised of women only, women, because of their direct interest, play a major role. Women were very important in the movement against the cost of living in Brazil in the 1970s, protesting government decisions that increased the cost of food. At about the same period, migrant women workers in Peru were organizing to demand land for their settlements, infrastructure services, and support for their initiatives, such as the *comedores populares* (community kitchens) in Lima. In the Caribbean, women have worked in trade unions to protest widespread poverty and government policies. In the late 1980s, women in Jamaica organized a consumer campaign to protest the high price of food while in Dominica they initiated a protest against the imposition of a sales tax on a wide range of essential goods.

In countries of Latin America, the strong presence of the Catholic Church at the community level often provided the institutional context within which women were able to organize and provide community services. In the Caribbean also, women organized in churches of various denominations, to reach out to the poor in the community and provide them with basic needs.[1] As a consequence, however, especially in Latin America, the church has exerted its own influence on the nature of their movements, serving to limit their challenge to government authority in some cases and in others to inhibit the discussion of crucial issues such as sexuality and reproductive rights, including abortion and family planning. Despite their suspicions of the feminist movement and their reluctance to be identified as feminist in the 1970s and 1980s, the women organized in these neighbourhood-based movements nevertheless managed, in several instances, to build alliances with the feminist groups, especially those with which they worked closely and in which they had the time and opportunity to develop confidence.

More recently women have pursued an alternate approach to social change—namely, feminism. During the 1970s and especially after the celebration of the first International Women's Day in Mexico in 1975 and the establishment of the International Decade for Women, 1975-1985, a great number of women, originally from the educated middle class, started to organize. They were not satisfied with improving their conditions of living but proposed a radical change in the way society organizes itself. Feminists first came together in informal discussion groups and voluntary organizations and later set up many more formal, non-profit organizations. They started by discussing the nature of the social-economic system in their countries and their shared situation as women, then organized to provide services that were not supplied by the state, including alternative health care and support for victims of sexual and domestic violence. Emergency women's groups providing shelter and advice proliferated in the region, enabling the women to establish important links with women in poor communities.

In the 1980s, these organized feminist groups, linked by their shared ideology of equality, freedom and transformative action, began to play a central role in challenging the dictatorships in many countries of Latin America and helped to bring about democratic processes. Inspired by the international women's movement, they brought to the political arena issues that until then were considered taboo or private issues, to be kept in the "sanctity" of the home. Under the slogan "the personal is political," they forced the incorporation in the political agenda of themes such as the invisibility of women's contribution to development, women's double work shifts, women's unpaid work in the home, sexuality, abortion, and reproductive rights, as well as domestic violence, sexual orientation and women's health.

As feminists and their organizations became more involved with the democratization movement, the critique of their middle-class origin forced them to be more inclusive, making an intentional effort to incorporate women from different social, cultural and ethnic backgrounds. The appeal for solidarity and sisterhood built in the common understanding of the situation of subordination that crossed different social and ethnic lines was the main engine in bringing them together. This was done without denying the differences that separate women inside the movement itself: rich women and poor, white and black and indigenous women, urban and rural women. The same was true in the Caribbean, where feminists' analysis of globalization and structural adjustment increasingly pushed them to ally with the poor and neighbourhood women who bore the brunt of these policies and who were dealing with them on a day-to-day basis. The Jamaica-based SISTREN, a working-class women's theatre collective, has used women's personal experiences to dramatize women's plight in culturally specific terms. It is not by coincidence that the most visible element in the Latin America and Caribbean Tent at the NGO Forum at the Fourth World Conference on Women in China in September 1995 was a banner proclaiming "Diversidad."

Despite their successes in community and non-governmental organizations (NGOs), both of these approaches have come up against obstacles to greater participation in the political arena, where women must compete directly with men. Few of the women community leaders, for example, have been included in the higher posts in the neighbourhood associations (generally reserved for men even when women engage in most of the mobilizing and lobbying efforts). And despite their increasing visibility on the international scene, feminists too are absent in the decision-making posts in local or national governments and parliaments.

There are exceptions: Benedita da Silva in Brazil, Piedad Cordoba in Colombia and Maria Antonieta Saa in Chile have made it, some from very poor origins, to the highest positions in parliament, where they become the necessary role models and important allies in the women's struggle for participation. But they remain exceptions. And in the Caribbean the record is equally sparse. The tradition of parliamentary democracy, inherited from the British, was more formal than participatory, discouraging grassroots leadership. Instead, several prominent women, notably the late Dame Nita Barrow in Barbados, have embodied the role of enlightened leader, providing important role models for other women. Dame Nita, who became her country's first female permanent representative to the United Nations, inspired women from all over the world when in 1985 she brought women from the first and third worlds together in the Peace Tent at the Third World Conference on Women in Nairobi. At her death in 1995, she was serving as Governor General of Barbados, the first woman to hold that position.

However, as the democratization process deepens in many countries along with the recognition of the inability of national governments to bring about change, a greater awareness of women's conditions and rights, and of women's success in achieving changes that increase their influence in the political process, may result in a revitalization of political parties. Examples can be seen in the guarantee of a minimum quota for women's candidates in elections in Costa Rica, Argentina and Brazil, and in similar efforts in the Dominican Republic. In addition, as women succeed in mobilizing voters around community and family issues, we can anticipate that political parties will begin to recruit more women community leaders for political careers.

Can Women Make a Difference?

As women's approaches to organizing for social change increasingly converge, whether in the various democratization movements or in efforts to combat the devastating impact of structural adjustment policies, feminists find themselves confronted with another apparent contradiction. While feminism is still premised on the principles of equality and the universality of human rights, feminists and activists increasingly recognize role-based differences between men and women and call attention to women's differential needs, perspectives and interests—in the family, the community, the workplace and society as a whole.

Differences that have to do with women's role in reproduction—maternal care, for instance—have been easily accepted, and even championed, as demanding specific attention. Far more controversial are gender-based differences that recall the stereotypes that feminists themselves have fought to abolish, such as, the idea that women by nature are more intuitive and nurturing, and thus less rational and competitive, than their male counterparts. The idea of enduring "feminine attributes" has been used, and is still being used, to justify the exclusion or the marginalization of women in society. The so-called masculine values of assertiveness, competitiveness and rationality have been seen as the qualities needed to run a business, manage a government office or to make decisions in congress, while so-called feminine qualities, such as nurturing and consensus building, have been seen as appropriate to home and family. Thus a great deal of women's efforts have been directed towards eliminating these stereotypes from classrooms and curriculums, textbooks, and the media in order to promote more egalitarian opportunities for women in society.

As women's presence in the public domain becomes more visible, however, the values long associated with "women's nature" have begun to take on a more positive association. The critique of authoritarian and hierarchical systems of organization, identified with a patriarchal order, become fertile ground for the favourable re-evaluation of so-called "women's attributes." Organizations of different kinds are now going through a process of "feminization" of their structures, some more rapidly and thoroughly than others, creating more space for the discussion and valuing of personal issues and problems, as well as reconsidering a more intuitive style of decision-making. Some of them are relying more on inclusive and horizontal schemes of power and responsibility. Team work and organization-wide communication processes are becoming common in business organizations and governments. (Contradictorily, however, the new hegemony of the market and the process of globalization of the economy seem to work in the opposite direction, concentrating power and weakening the basis of the social pyramid.)

Most feminists are aware of the danger inherent in such an approach - namely, the reestablishment of the very stereotypes that have served both to define and to marginalize them for centuries. They argue that the qualities considered to be female, now being revalued, are not based in biology, as proponents assert, but arise from conditions in society that still exist. Thus, they maintain, because women have historically been excluded from decision-making they do not benefit from, and in fact have no commitment to, the model of development that has brought the world to an unbearable situation of crisis—comprising an ecological crisis, a crisis of economic imbalance and poverty, and a crisis of war and conflict. Therefore, given the opportunity, and sufficient support, they (not one or two women isolated in a hostile male environment) will make decisions that will challenge this path of development.

An extension of this argument applies to women's leadership in general. Its proponents maintain that due to a different process of socialization, women, at this point in the history of humanity, have developed the personal qualities that are required to bring development to the right path of democracy, justice and peace, as well as sustainability. They are seen, and see themselves, as less hierarchical, more inclusive, more process oriented, more caring in terms of individual personal needs and more willing to make sacrifices in favour of their family, community or society's well-being.

Studies of and interest in the issue of possible different styles of exerting power and management are beginning to call the attention of the women in the region.[2] They are aware that studies and research done in the North have identified differences between men and women, especially in positions of authority in the private sector, but that there is some evidence to suggest these differences diminish as women become more accustomed to management positions. Theory aside, how well has feminism done in practice?

In the United States, during the heady days of feminism's "second wave" in the 1970s, women also believed they could change the world—or at least make a difference. Once women had access to decision-making positions, they assumed they would be able to transform their organizations and make society a better place for everyone, especially those traditionally excluded from power and resources. A 1976 study of women state and federal congressional candidates, for example, found that "an overwhelming majority of women candidates" felt they could do a better job of representing "women's interests" than their male counterparts.

Today, though they still believe they will change the world, they realize it is more complicated than they thought. And more long-term. Although women now make up a significant number of the CEOs of U.S. companies, they still do not head any Fortune 500 companies; similarly, the foundations they control are generally the smaller ones; women head up less than a quarter of those with assets over $100 million. And women have discovered that alone at the top, they can do little; their ability to bring about significant change depends on being part of a "critical mass"— of more women in leadership positions. In the corporate sector, this means women must comprise a greater percentage of senior management; in the non-profit sector, it means women must also be on boards of directors. Without this critical mass, corporate and bureaucratic structures combine with a workplace culture that has either been more friendly to men or that has obliged men to adapt; in it, women feel themselves marginalized and unable to bring about significant change.[3]

In politics, where women are expected to have a woman's agenda, it may be easier: thus women in state legislatures have worked across party lines on issues such as child care, pay and pension equity, rape, marital and divorce law, and domestic violence. Drawing on support for such issues among voting women, they feel confident in confronting male opposition. In a 1981 survey, a majority of women officeholders at state and federal levels said they specifically sought out women for staff positions. Yet even in politics, younger women appointees are described as "ambitious professional politicians, cautious game-players toeing the line, careful about alienating the men in power."[4]

Looking more narrowly at organizational change, there is a growing body of literature on women's "styles" of management, which posit a more consensual, collaborative approach to decision-making than the hierarchical approach attributed to men. To the extent that this difference is true, it is interesting to consider the reasons behind it. A recent survey of women in top management positions in the U.S. private sector revealed that second to stamina, the single most important requirement was that they adjust their personal styles so as not to threaten their male colleagues. And a 1991 study of women CEOs in U.S. foundations revealed that the higher the position, the more cautious the occupant, raising questions about the effective use of power in order to advocate for social change.[5]

Perhaps equally significant, however, are the paths women take to leadership, which are often quite different from those of men. With few opportunities for leadership or promotion in the private sector, women often acquire decision-making skills and experience through their activities in the volunteer sector, where achieving broad consensus is necessarily more important. As long as women's opportunities remain restricted therefore, we may expect to see enduring differences in leadership styles.

Moreover, since the late 1970s, in the United States as well as in Latin America and the Caribbean, much of women's managerial experience has taken place in women's organizations, which distinguish themselves from private sector organizations in the way they conceptualize power relationships. Striving to embody the notion of "sisterhood" in their own organizations, the organizations that women formed in the 1970s and early 1980s stressed values of participation and consensus, as well as a more flexible work style. While formal hierarchy could be eliminated, informal hierarchy could, and frequently did, take its place, especially as the groups expanded, and these informal structures were made worse by the fact that they were obscured by the prevailing principles of equality and consensus.

During the 1980s especially, feminists started to create new organizations that could serve as a basis for their activism. The circumstances were favourable. International donors provided most of the required funding. Governments were beginning to use their expertise and contacts with grassroots women to reach out with services.6 NGOs, and women's groups in particular, began to proliferate throughout Latin America and the Caribbean. At the same time, part of their goal was to transcend the limits of the individual organizations by establishing links with several overlapping networks at the local, national, regional and international level. While this proved to be an excellent strategy in strengthening their positions and ability to influence the political process, especially at the international level, it did not enable them to deal with the problem of sustainability—a problem now being faced by groups and organizations throughout the region.

The Quest for Survival

Throughout the region, women's organizations have gone through many changes, devising ever new survival strategies as they adjust to changing economic and political climates. During the 1980s, however, as interest in NGOs flowered and international support allowed women's organizations to become more professionally structured, creating permanent jobs, some of them full time, women in these organizations began to think about survival differently. As a result they confronted new problems, very different from those when they were loose groupings of voluntary activist women, each one of them caring individually for their subsistence needs, and meeting in kitchens and living rooms and school rooms around the country. Women's NGOs now face the tasks of mobilizing a stable flow of financial and human resources and acquiring the expertise to manage them. Resources should be enough to allow for the maintenance of the organization (space, administration, communication, etc.) and for the delivery of its products.

At the same time as the number of NGOs increases, potential funding sources are shrinking. Women's NGOs now must compete with each other for available resources. Many of them are now established organizations, more than a decade old. In the recent past, during the economic crisis of the 1980s, international donors reached out to organizations in the region, eager to be a part of efforts to rebuild civil society. As a result, many women's organizations became an attractive employment alternative for activist women. Today, however, new priorities as well as the aggravation of old ones distract the donor community away from the region.

The Cold War was accompanied by the fear that the region could fall prey to the communist ideology, a fear that in the 1970s and 1980s helped to attract resources to the region. Throughout Latin America, right-wing dictatorships have collapsed and the left-wing national or socialist liberation movements seem to have either incorporated themselves into the democratic process or to be sufficiently under the control of the national government in most countries that they are no longer a threat. Despite the fact that poverty has increased in the period, penalizing women more than proportionally, the region has started to exhibit some positive indicators of (aggregated) economic growth. Some of the countries in the region are comparable to developed ones in terms of quality of life indicators. Even so, in many cases such indicators are more formal than real, and such gains as have been made are increasingly jeopardized as structural adjustment policies begin to bite, especially in the Caribbean. At the same time, the collapse of the Soviet Union created a new concern for the stability of the former countries of the Soviet bloc, notably those in Eastern Europe. These so-called Countries in Transition (to free-market capitalism) are now a great interest of the donor community, pulling resources away from Latin America and the Caribbean.

Feeling the impact of these trends, women's NGOs throughout the Caribbean and Latin America have started to explore alternatives that could guarantee their survival as relevant organizations of the women's movement.

Balancing Feminist Principles and Efficiency

Women's NGOs have been created as a way to put into practice egalitarian values based on women's solidarity and partnership. The same values that are being proposed for the entire society are expected to apply internally. As these organizations begin to grow and to interact, in a more systematic way, with new partners outside the women's movement, they confront the need for greater efficiency. International donors and governments who supply most of the resources also demand quality projects, periodic evaluation, substantive reports and accountability. All of this requires a more institutionalized internal division of labour, mechanisms for quality control of processes, products and performances, good public relations. Perhaps even more important, they oblige the organizations to define how power and decision-making are distributed internally.

NGOs are currently trying to accommodate this new perspective within the framework of organizational structures that stress the values of democracy and participation, where power is expected to be widely shared and where each member is encouraged to perceive herself as having an equal share in the ownership of the whole organization.

While research into how women's NGOs in the region are adjusting to the new circumstances is just beginning, it is evident from what we already know that a complex and difficult process is taking place, sometimes dividing organizations. The charismatic leaders who typically created women's NGOs and were responsible for their expansion are being challenged by newly recruited professionals who have different styles of leadership even when pursuing similar goals. Some leaders have decided to leave after years of dedication, opening the question of what criteria should be adopted in choosing new leadership. Such things as flexible hours, which represent an intentional gender-sensitive response to women's multiple roles, are under scrutiny. How can the organization balance flexibility with the need for more reliable and predictable work processes and outputs?

Although some of the problems faced are common to all organizations, especially to non-profit organizations, some are particular to feminist organizations, which have as their goal the transformation of society according to parameters of equality, justice and peace. The ways in which these organizations resolve these dilemmas can offer an important contribution to the future of organizations and to the betterment of life in general.

Women in Leadership: Case Studies

Until there is a significant body of research on women's leadership, both over time and in a cross-cultural context, case studies of the many projects devoted to developing and making women's leadership visible play an important role in our understanding of this complex subject. The four case studies in this book are designed to fill that role. Each describes a project supported by UNIFEM in the belief that the best way to help women in developing countries is to strengthen the organizations they create and control, while fostering links and the sharing of experiences at all levels. Together they embrace insights derived from both currents of the women's movement and many aspects of their experience. Thus Meryl James Sebro writes about grassroots women finding their own voices as a means to empowerment in the Rose Hall community organizing project in St. Vincent in the Caribbean. The study documents the emergence of rural women, who through the process of strategic engagement, empowered themselves to effect positive change in their community, even to the point of challenging political and government leadership. Sonia de Avelar and Gina Zabludovsky describe the barriers to leadership that professional and managerial women encounter and strive to overcome as they hit the glass ceiling in corporate and governmental organizations. Throughout the region, although women are beginning to move into management and leadership positions, they face the same limitations in both the private and public sector; they tend to cluster in low- and mid-level administrative positions, predominate in low-paying industries and trades, and rank low in credit-worthiness. They are also virtually excluded from employers association boards and decision making committees, limiting their access to promotion. Based on research on women in professional and managerial jobs as well as business owners in Brazil and Mexico, the authors identify the gender-related barriers (attitudinal, organizational and institutional) that prevent women's advancement in both countries as well as the different possibilities for change in each.

Two case studies focus on women's experience in the organizations they have built themselves. Delaine Martins Costa and Gleisi Heisler Neves describe a process of evaluation and reassessment in two well-known feminist organizations—the Women's Education Network (Rede Mulher de Educacão) in Brazil and the Flora Tristan Centre in Peru—as they attempt to expand and consolidate their position after 20 years of existence. Both of them are currently reorganizing to accommodate feminist principles with organizational efficiency in a new vision of leadership. Finally Lucero Gonzalez and Joanne Sandler look at the experience of the Sociedad Mexicana pro Derechos de la Mujer in Mexico as a case study of the growing effort to make all women's organizations—and the transformative principles that they embody—sustainable through the creation of national women's funding movements. Throughout the region, as feminists look at the organizations they have created and ask how they can become more sustainable, they strive to keep hold of their original vision. ❖

---

1 In some places, notably Haiti and Cuba, women have also drawn on "folk" religions, such as voudon and santeria, for a source of women power and resistance.

2 See, for instance, IBAM/Ministerio de Asuntos Sociales – Instituto de la Mujer, *Genero y Desarollo Institutional en Ongs,* Rio de Janeiro, IBAM, 1995, passim.

3 Women's networks have been important here, helping to identify qualified women for boards and commissions as well as jobs. Yet a little-discussed tendency to pull the ladder up behind them may operate against women ever achieving the needed critical mass.

4 See Ruth Mandel, "The Political Woman," in Sara Rix, ed., *The American Woman* 1988-89 (New York: Norton, 1988).

5 See Catalyst, "Women in Corporate Leadership: Program and Prospects," 1996 and Women and Foundations/Corporate Philanthropy, "Making a Difference: The Impact of Women in Philanthropy," 1991.

6 The relationship between governments and women's NGOs is not easy as women fight to maintain their autonomy, and government tries to neutralize their protests or make the "best use" of them. As women began to have access to decision-making positions in government this relationship becomes even more complex, as women must constrain their activities within very tight limits.

Empowering Women for Community Leadership: A Caribbean Case Study

MERYL JAMES SEBRO

"Above all, she has a voice, one which she uses to articulate her own needs and create more space for herself and others without power, thus demonstrating a fundamental characteristic of leadership: the ability to include the powerless."

The drastic downturn in the Caribbean economy blew in during the 1980s like the hurricane no one expected or wanted, challenging the time-worn folk wisdom that "no bad wind does blow." Falling exports, increasing inflation, capital flight, and rapidly escalating public debt resulted in rising unemployment and plummeting wages. A corresponding increase in the cost of basic needs, a reduction in social services, and increasing health problems caused by improper industrial and environmental management dumped heavier burdens on the already overburdened poor. In addition, structural adjustment policies imposed by the international lending agencies in an effort to rein in "excessive" social spending wreaked further havoc on the poor, most of whom are women. It was thus left to the women, in the face of the failure of these policies, to pick up the slack in caring for the sick, the children, the elderly, and their menfolk. Women must now employ creative and productive strategies—both inside and outside of the home—in order to generate income to ensure the survival of their households and the welfare of their communities.

In spite of their Herculean feats in this regard, still today, in the middle of the 1990s, the contribution of women is rarely factored into national development plans. Moreover, women's issues continue to be perceived by male planners as pertaining primarily to children and social welfare. But women themselves have begun to look at issues that concern them and their families through lenses that are more clearly focused on social, economic and political changes that are directly linked to national planning and development goals and strategies. In their view, male-dominated governments have become more unreliable as government policies, however externally influenced, continue to fail, and their own pain, poverty and powerlessness surpass the level with which they were all too familiar.

Drawing on historical traditions of leadership, collective responsibility, sharing and interdependence, women have expanded their strategies for survival into the community, and are seeking to make deeper inroads into national planning and implementation. While a few women have attained high-level positions in government and the private sector, they are the exceptions, not the rule. Constraints at the community and local levels have now forced women to a greater understanding of the importance and function of leadership, compelling them to push past traditional gender, spatial and socioeconomic boundaries in order to shift their focus to political and government involvement. In so doing they must confront head-on several issues and attitudes, old and new, which must be negotiated in order to pursue their mission. Added to these are unprecedented levels of violence against women as well as rampant crime, which restricts women's mobility.

Central to women's ability to negotiate these new challenges is empowerment. Women attain empowerment in removing themselves from behind masks of helplessness, hopelessness and voicelessness to become engaged in problem identification as well as problem solution; project planning as well as project implementation, and to embark upon a process of consensus-building in an attempt to direct this new-found confidence and visibility into policy formulation, as well as policy support.

Women's empowerment is accompanied by unsettling perceptions of empowered women, since empowered behaviour, while considered professional in men, for women carries a perception of aggressiveness and masculinity, or worse, a desperate need of a man. Ironically, many women share these perceptions, making the task of empowering themselves doubly difficult. Even so, they have begun. While their input in charting the direction of their countries has been minimal, this is primarily because gender has not been placed as a central issue in development planning.

Another, related issue is the devaluation of women's time and labour. This issue becomes especially critical as women move from the private sphere of the home into the public sphere of the community and the wider society. While there is a need for greater research in this area, there appears to be a fundamental difference in leadership styles of women and men, which allows men to focus on, and concentrate on, policy issues. Women, on the other hand, often get sidelined with issues of personality and run the risk of losing focus and marginalizing their own interests. This tendency leaves women particularly vulnerable to divisive strategies by men as well as women.

It is in the context of all of these issues that UNIFEM has been supporting recent efforts by women's NGOs in the region to define their own space, act on their own agenda, and through the process of engagement to empower themselves to assume the mantle of leadership. The case study of Rose Hall documents the activities of one women's community group to effect change in their community, which then spread to other communities in the country and indeed has begun to influence attitudes and approaches to development and change throughout the Caribbean.

The Rose Hall Experience

Perched high on the northwest corner of St. Vincent some 1,232 feet above sea level is the farming community of Rose Hall with a population of 1,500. Half of the population is under 30 years old. Battling the problems of poverty, high unemployment, low wages from agriculture (the community's primary income earner), inadequate facilities, large families, and a growing idle youth population, Rose Hall presented an ideal location for the testing of a strategy and methodology for mobilizing women's leadership at the community level. The women of Rose Hall, who have forged a tradition of self-reliance through cooperation from a history of surviving hurricanes and volcanic eruptions, exhibited tremendous potential for leadership. They were an ideal group with which to test a process concerned with participation, empowerment and community self-reliance.

In 1980, the Women and Development Unit (WAND) of the School of Continuing Studies at the University of the West Indies designed a pilot project, Communities Organizing for Self-Reliance (CORE), to empower women and counter marginalization in the rural sector. WAND seeks to expand information exchange among women in communities in order to increase their options and awareness of new ideas and methodologies. The two main elements of the CORE process are:

- strengthening of community organizations with the specific aim of empowering poor women in rural communities

- challenging the prevailing development models and policies, which are influenced by market-driven forces outside the region, with the aim of formulating and pursuing an alternative development model that does not foster discrimination on the bases of gender, race, class and religion.

The basic CORE strategy is to work through a local NGO or NGOs in each community. CORE is currently working with NGOs in 14 communities in seven countries in the Caribbean. The community of Rose Hall was the first to be introduced to the CORE programme, including its commitment to the empowerment of women as an integral part of the concept of sustainable development. After consultations among themselves, the leaders of existing community organizations agreed to participate and so began the long, slow process of empowerment. UNIFEM support facilitated the consolidation of the process in Rose Hall, which participated in the process for the longest duration, as well as streamlining of the process in the other six participating Caribbean countries.

In Rose Hall, the objectives of community mobilization and organizational strengthening were based on a participatory methodology in the areas of needs assessment, programme planning and decision-making. A Rose Hall Working Group was established to spearhead the project. Women and some men in the community were selected from existing community organizations and were mobilized for training. The approach to organizational strengthening included data gathering about the community. Initial workshops were held on community-needs assessment, out of which came workshops on programme planning and evaluation, followed by workshops on personal development and leadership, and skills training in analytical methods, including gender analysis. Income-earning projects were designed and implemented. Technical assistance was provided in the form of planning guidance, organizational analysis and development and evaluation, as well as specialized skills training: updated farm management techniques; food preservation; garment manufacturing; and small-business management. Apart from those specific areas of technical assistance, all other activities were executed by the community members themselves.

Special efforts were made to move participation beyond Rose Hall to include fieldworkers from various agencies in other communities. The Working Group identified, analyzed and prioritized the needs of the community, and proposed solutions. Rose Hall members agreed on several projects, as well as on the persons to manage them. Although the result was the empowering of the entire community, four women emerged as notable leaders [names have been changed for subjects' protection]: Viola Staples, who reassessed her natural leadership abilities and from a "mere housewife" developed into the overall project leader, national and international troubleshooter, irrepressible spokesperson and role model; Esther Walters, who used her training and experience as an educator to manage a pre-school project and to confront the Ministry of Education in the interest of the community; Sandra Winsome, who threw off her shyness to whip into shape a bakery project, squeezing out profits in the face of persistent creditors; and Belle Cleveland, who inspired by her leadership experience in the adult literacy programme sought advanced training overseas and returned as a regional consultant*. For these four women, as for the entire community, the key to empowerment and community leadership was self-confidence based on knowledge, self-esteem based on action.

Viola Staples: Project Manager

The success of the CORE project in Rose Hall can perhaps best be captured in the words of Viola Staples. A Rose Hall participant from the very inception of the project, she casually illustrates a fundamental focus of gender analysis, that of the devaluation of women's time and labour:

> I was just a mere housewife, a farmer, a baker, a seamstress...all things. But you know what happen? I never really realize that all of these things that I had were "skills," you know. I didn't realize this until...in the 1981 workshop these things became real...real, real, real to me, that I been baking cakes for years! I've been trying to do my own little thing, cut out the neck of my dress and sew it up and so on. I didn't really realize that these things is really "skills" that I have. And even talking to people, I didn't realize that is a skill I have. And now what is happening? I does talk too much now! I find that sometimes I does talk too much now...and all because of this project here.

The person that Viola Staples is speaks reams for the courage, determination, resilience and leadership skills of today's Caribbean women

---

* *Names of persons quoted have been changed.*

as they push through the barriers that have historically limited and devalued their contributions and made them invisible. Today's Viola is confident, self-assured and brimming with self-esteem, creativity and self-assurance. Above all, she has a voice, one which she uses to articulate her own needs and create more space for herself and others without power, thus demonstrating a fundamental characteristic of leadership: the ability to include the powerless.

Today's Viola has repackaged and marketed her skills in order not only to increase her own earning power, but to assist others in doing the same.

> I have turned my skills into making money for myself, in helping people to make money, in helping people to also realize that they too have values, that they too have potentials that they could use...helping to make people happy. So now I am using those skills to help others in the island of St. Vincent and the Grenadines...in the whole world...and that is why UNIFEM must send the money for us.

Viola Staples is not alone. She is one of several women who, though neophytes at the inception of the CORE project, have had ample opportunity to exercise the fundamental principles of community collaboration, self-reliance and participation. When the need for a community building was identified—one of the first needs to be identified through the CORE project—the community pooled its human resources and began the work on the foundation. But a change of government dictated a change of attitude and support for the project, and the community received word that work must be stopped so that the relevant ministry could finish the building itself. Government funding was frozen and the group instructed to cease work on the structure. The community sent a delegation to express its dissatisfaction but was further discouraged with the response of the official, who strongly advised that his directive be followed. Rose Hall agreed to stop work on the structure. When the community felt that enough time had passed, they sent another delegation, comprising four women; but this time they went over the head of the government official directly to the country's prime minister. The situation was immediately resolved, government again made funds available and construction on the building resumed.

The Rose Hall Community Centre now stands proudly as concrete evidence of the possibilities of leadership and engagement...identifying community needs and ensuring that these needs are integrated into national development planning. The critical involvement of women did not go unnoticed. "When we do these things and we see results, it keeps building our confidence that things could happen," says Viola with a determined smile. Noting the spin-off effects of their confrontation with national government, Viola explains, "Seeing these things happened, people themselves gained confidence."

Esther Walters: Pre-School Project Coordinator

Esther Walters is a 50-something home economics teacher, now acting principal of a secondary school, and a project participant from its inception. When the community identified the need for a pre-school, naturally Esther was considered one of the point persons. Her increased self-confidence is rooted in the ability to tackle problems and reap solutions from seeming insurmountable situations. For example, the community experienced unexpected opposition from school officials when they attempted to use a classroom in the primary school for housing the pre-school, simply because there was no historical precedent. There was, however, a precedent the women of Rose Hall had already established of meeting directly with government officials in order to surmount bureaucratic hurdles.

When community meetings with school officials failed to change their position, letters were sent to the Ministry of Education. A series of follow-up community meetings brought about a decision to send a delegation to the ministry. Sensing that she might be able to avoid confrontation, Esther, on her own initiative, paid a visit to the chief education officer and advised him that a visit from the Rose Hall delegation was imminent, since they were not satisfied with the response from the ministry. The chief education officer acted promptly to avoid the impending danger. He and several ministry officials paid a visit to Rose Hall. The space was soon granted for the pre-school, which still operates. As Esther concluded from this experience:

> We see *within* our community. We knew what our needs were, we saw a way of solving it, we followed a particular process, and it worked. That happened, so it gave us—me, specifically—greater self-confidence, confidence that we could get what we ask for, if we know how to do it. It's the know-how.

It is for this reason that project participants particularly laud the impact of CORE on education in the village. An adult education programme, initiated in 1981, still continues. It focuses on literacy, academics, vocational skills training and specialized skills training that includes garment making, food preservation and the management of economic enterprises. The programme includes group discussions on current issues; the pre-school programme includes special training for mothers in nutrition, parenting and early childhood training; and the Farmers Group exposes farmers to updated farming practices as well as academic research in agriculture.

Sandra Winsome, Bakery Project Coordinator

The pilot project also spawned a bakery as a service-rendering sub-project, after a survey identified its need. Rose Hall now not only supplies its community with fresh bread daily, but "exports" bread to neighbouring communities. Again, the project has produced spin-offs to other communities, which felt, "If Rose Hall has this and it's working, we can try too." Hence, other communities have instituted pre-schools and adult literacy programmes, with technical assistance from Rose Hall members.

The coordinator of the bakery, Sandra Winsome, is one of the younger and more recent members of the Rose Hall Working Group and fully represents the continuity of the impact of the project after 15 years. At age 27, Sandra describes herself as "shy and sometimeish" even after two years in England studying to become a secretary. Project workshops have filled her with more self-confidence, however, so that she is now able to "go brave and say anything I want." And even though she admits that sometimes she still gets scared, she is now able to talk before crowds. She says she is "self-reliant and empowered" so that she does not flinch when people come to the bakery and try to bully her into giving them free bread by saying "naughty things."

> I don't take notice of them. I understand people more, so when I hear people saying all those things, I know that I am doing my job, so I don't even bother. I tell them that the bakery is for us to make money and if I give everybody one bread, there wouldn't be any bread (to sell)."

Sandra has taken an equally firm grip of her life. She has a boyfriend, and although many of her friends who are not married have children, she has no intention of having children outside of marriage. Her training in self-reliance and self-confidence, as well as the support received from other members of the group, have empowered her to make carefully thought-out choices and take control of her life.

Belle Cleveland: Adult Literacy Programme

Perhaps the surprise fringe benefit of the CORE project is the outward and upward mobility that it affords its participants. Belle Cleveland was a young school teacher in her 20s when the programme began, so the leadership role for the adult literacy programme became her responsibility. Five years later, in 1986, the government saw the need to implement a similar programme at the national level. Belle applied for and got the position of coordinator of the country's national adult literacy programme in the Ministry of Education. This spurred her on to obtain advanced degrees in continuing education and development studies. Currently she is a consultant to the Rose Hall project and to the CORE project in St. Lucia.

Participants of the Rose Hall Working Group have also migrated from Rose Hall to spread their talents elsewhere. This outward movement itself is considered a measure of accomplishment and improvement, since community residents have historically remained in Rose Hall because they felt that they did not possess the necessary skills to compete on the outside. The project has also given birth to small enterprises, as members who had received training and had honed specific skills took over project ideas and turned them into income-earning businesses for themselves and others. The bakery project provides baked goods for Rose Hall and surrounding communities, as well as income for its workers. The garment-making project is now in the hands of a group member who has turned it into a thriving business providing school uniforms for children and a livelihood for himself and the community members employed, most of whom are women. Similarly, the food-preservation project has spurred many community women to support their families by producing and marketing bottled seasonings.

The group must now come to terms with new directions as social needs translate into economic challenges. Recognizing its limitations and lack of resources as a large-scale employer, its aim is to train and provide jobs for a few more people, who can then provide jobs for a few more. Aware that this new direction is taking place in an environment of scarce internal resources and reduced external funding, under Belle Cleveland's leadership the group has begun to review its own management structure in order "to become more efficient, competitive, and innovative in maximizing existing resources."

Redefining Leadership

Women in Rose Hall now feel they have a say in where they belong—both at the community and the national levels. They have had an impact on national planning and helped determine the direction of their community. They also have a sense of belonging at the regional level, where they have provided technical assistance for similar projects elsewhere in the region. The women of Rose Hall are being seen and heard.

With her newly found voice, Viola Staples loudly declares:

> In 1980-81, if somebody had told me that I would have been the person that I am today, I would tell have said no. Because I couldn't see me, I couldn't see this piece of flesh here coming or being what I am. Because the opportunity wasn't there for me. And when the opportunity came, although I wanted to do it, I was still thinking that I would not be able to do it right.

But Viola Staples, and those like her in Rose Hall and throughout the Caribbean are doing it right, emerging from the cobwebs of invisibility. Rose Hall is one of the villages leading the island, perhaps even the region, in community development. Viola Staples herself has taken her leadership skills to a position of national impact, serving as a government fieldworker in the Ministry of Housing and Community Development. Like Belle Cleveland, who now serves as project consultant, Viola Staples, Esther Walters and Sandra Winsome have assumed major leadership roles in the project, ensuring that what they have learned and become is transmitted to the young people in the community, the next generation of leaders.

Part of the success of the Rose Hall project lies in its long-term existence. Its viability and longevity demonstrate the importance of instituting intensive leadership-training programmes in order to prepare women for the new leadership roles to which they are being called. Credit must be given as well to the mix of participating women, who ranged from barely literate to professional; who saw the need for change, and were willing to help effect it; but more significantly, who were ready to support and assist each other in the process. "That is what development is all about," offers Viola Staples. Development is not that I know it all...what I say goes, you are going to sit down and listen to me. Development is not like that. It is each one teach one something. You learn from me and I learn from you. Development is a building of trust in each other."

Esther Walters agrees: "There must be participation from as many as possible. Everybody. You listen to what people have to say. You have to listen. Regardless of how small, or how large, or how maybe illiterate, or what you think somebody might be, that person could have a gold mine of experiences and something to offer. You don't have all the say. You have to listen and take advice from other people."

Part of this process of readiness might be the preparation of a comprehensive alternative economic-development document that specifically includes and elaborates four major areas: gender, culture, the environment, and entrepreneurial development. Such a document would not only assist women in political leadership but could be adopted by the women's movement and urged upon governments throughout the region.

The case of Rose Hall in St. Vincent, perhaps because of its long life, presents the most dramatic example of leadership through empowerment. There the women were able to identify the changes in themselves, to re-evaluate their own skills, their lives and their potential contribution to society directly as a result of the CORE project. The validity of the concept of unwaged labour in the family and community and the critical importance of putting a value on women's productive and reproductive time were reinforced by Viola Staples' discovery of her self-worth, once she learned in her workshop that the things she did every day were skills and began to demand their inclusion in national development planning. In addition, the Rose Hall women were able to identify the positive impact of their activities on neighbouring communities, and, in fact, saw as a major responsibility and commitment the passing on of their skills to other communities and to young people, both male and female.

At a deeper level, the emergence of new women leaders such as Viola Staples, Esther Walters, Sandra Winsome and Belle Cleveland has challenged male-defined concepts of leadership. The engagement, emergence, and empowerment of these women demand an examination of the degree to which the lack of recognition of women's management in the private sphere (home) negatively influences development planning in the public sphere. There is the unspoken but pervasive male terror that to validate women's power in the home by acknowledging it in the public domain will sound a death knell to male dominance. Failure to do so, however, is to deprive society of the invaluable contribution of women, who represent the life force of their societies. In addition, national statistics fail to factor in their contribution and hence short-change development planning from the very beginning by failing to draw on women's resources, knowledge, experience, leadership, and yes, intuition.

The necessary translation of women's domestic economic autonomy into political autonomy in the wider society is inextricably linked to the re-evaluation of women's time and labour, both inside and outside the home. In order to bring this about, women must acquire an economic base outside the home, enabling them to take their place at the decision-making and planning levels.

The Rose Hall experience in St. Vincent demonstrates that once women remove the mask of invisibility, there is no stopping them nor the benefits that accrue to the wider community. The ability to share successes and to expand benefits beyond the immediate boundaries of projects emerge as a specific characteristic of female leadership. Rose Hall women intend to include young men when they pass on the skills they have learned. Already they serve as advisors to communities that are developing similar projects.

What also emerges is a leadership style that is as concerned with the journey as it is with the destination; that considers a process that focuses on consensus-building and shared power of equal importance to achieving desired goals. In addition there is a sense of equal participation and egalitarianism that places equal value on the input of the more experienced leaders, such as Viola Staples, as on the young, shy and insecure, such as Sandra Winsome. The leadership style is characterized by patience, support and encouragement, which created a nurturing environment for the blossoming of Sandra Winsome, as well as for the reassessment and validation of the skills of Viola Staples. Guided by a spirit of collaboration, Esther Walters could initiate a confrontation with the ministry, knowing that her action would be supported, and Belle Cleveland could apply her Rose Hall experience to a national-level literacy project. The passing of the baton from Staples, herself involved in national-level projects, and the clearly articulated goal of preparing the next generation of leaders indicate an understanding of the crucial importance of succession planning, with the specific intent of including the powerless. "But even though I pass on to the great beyond," Staples says, "I have a firm belief that the projects are going to continue, and other projects are going to develop for the betterment of Rose Hall."

The emphasis on opening the playing field, the concern for each other's personal lives as it impacts on the progress of the project, which came naturally to Rose Hall women, characterizes women's leadership and can be placed under the banner of "total quality management" now pursued as a corporate ideal. Self-reliance and self-confidence, however, remain fundamental to empowerment. Viola Staples is confident that with help from UNIFEM, she is ready and able to help the whole world. Prophetically, in 1987, she addressed world leaders at the United Nations, where she directed them to hold hands and sing the Rose Hall theme song. The lyrics, reproduced here, were written by members of the group:

"The time has come
when we must share
and to assist in any way
So let us join in unity
To build our community
Oh! What a village this will be
With benefits for you and me
If time and talents we will give
To build our community."

The resourcefulness through which women have won a degree of economic autonomy in the home provides the basis for coping and survival strategies for the community, and eventually for the entire society. Since women are the primary transmitters of culture, the merging of the economic and the cultural sectors becomes a tangible fringe benefit of women's leadership. In Trinidad and Tobago, for example, when women failed to gain access to start-up funding for micro-enterprises, they "blanked" the banks and formal financial institutions and formed a susu, an informal economic arrangement, in order to raise funds for their businesses. In so doing, these women returned to an indigenous solution, one used by their ancestors to counter similar economic frustrations. They knew the solution was viable because they had used it successfully in managing their own households.

Within post-colonial societies, if not everywhere, women appear to have a greater tendency to apply internal solutions, rooted in culture and history, to seemingly external problems, perhaps because their experience of culture has been less tainted by external cultural pollutants. This inward search for solutions is an important and much ignored aspect of development, and represents a fertile area for alternative development strategies. It represents a resource that could be of particular assistance to male dominated governments, which have historically relied on externally directed solutions for national development problems. In the Caribbean in particular, currently in the midst of a social, economic, and political crisis brought about largely through the application of external solutions to internal problems, this area seems ripe for exploration.

Because of this, women throughout the region must place their own political empowerment firmly on their own agenda, in order that Caribbean communities can develop into societies that are equitable, just and mature enough to engage all of their human resources during a dramatic and traumatic period of change. At least for Rose Hall, the winds of change have blown in new hope, a deeper consciousness of gender and an awareness that with training and opportunities, possibilities are limitless. Moreover, it has brought the Rose Hall women face to face with the challenge of perceiving the profit motive as something other than capitalist greed; namely, as a strategy for economic empowerment, and through it, for project sustainability and community survival. ❖

Women's Leadership and Glass Ceiling Barriers in Brazil and Mexico

SONIA DE AVELAR AND GINA ZABLUDOVSKY

"Untested assumptions about women's commitment and abilities underlie corporate culture, policies and practices, and create a work environment that reduces women's opportunity for the practical experiences necessary for advancement.."

Women in Latin America and the Caribbean have made impressive gains in both education and employment since the 1970s. In line with international trends, female economic activity rates increased, as did the ratio of women to men in the economically active population. In the 1990s, women have actually outnumbered men in higher education in many countries, as shown by the average rate of female enrollment in tertiary education (51.4 percent). And in the last two decades women have also increased their numbers in traditional male domains, such as university enrollment in science and technology, and in law and business careers (44.4 percent and 53.4 percent, respectively).

In the business world, the representation of women in management has grown steadily, rising to 45.9 percent in 1990 (from 33.3 percent in 1970), and according to a UN survey on the role of women in development, the region had on average the highest rate of women in administrative and managerial jobs in the 1980s.[1] Moreover, women make up an increasing percentage of small-business owners and employers, a fact of economic life that is only beginning to be acknowledged. The sense is that in the universe of micro/small businesses, women may comprise nearly half of the entrepreneurs. As they have increased their participation in income-generating activities, moreover, women have come to constitute a large share of the consumer markets in the region as well.

However, despite these significant gains, the playing field is still far from level for women in competing for opportunities and access to resources. The wide gaps between women's educational achievements and large-scale entry into business careers on the one hand and their status in management and in business ownership on the other points to sharp inequalities in opportunities and treatment. Throughout the region, although women are moving into management and entrepreneurship at a faster pace than men, they are rarely found in the upper strata of managerial occupations or on corporate boards. They tend to cluster in low and mid-level administrative positions, to predominate in low-paying industries and trades, and rank low in creditworthiness. Being virtually excluded from employers' associations, boards and decision-making committees, their access to promotion in both the private and the public sector is still limited. These circumstances are reflected in wage differentials; the managerial and executive salary gap between men and women can reach 50 percent, as illustrated by estimated average incomes in those occupations for five selected cities in the region.[2]

Despite this reality, however, little is known or understood about the gender-related barriers (attitudinal, organizational and institutional) that prevent women's advancement in management and business. Accordingly, UNIFEM supported research on "Women in Decision-making in Latin America: A Glass Ceiling Report." The study focuses on women in management and business in Brazil and Mexico, the region's largest economies. The goal was not only to assess the current status of women in business and management and identify opportunities for their advancement but also to build public awareness on factors that limit women's ability advance in business careers in the region.

Research in a number of countries in the world has identified a glass ceiling, "those invisible artificial barriers based on attitudinal and organizational biases" that keep qualified women from rising in organizations, as a determinant of women's lack of professional advancement or career derailment.[3] Cultural codes (sex stereotypes) about female abilities, their capacity for decision-making or risk-taking, their degree of professional commitment or need to balance career and family responsibilities, their willingness to relocate, as well as assumptions that clients hold "negative" attitudes towards female directors, act as obstacles in the recruitment, retention and promotion of women, in spite of their educational credentials. These untested assumptions about women's abilities and commitment underlie corporate culture, policies and practices, and create a work environment that denies women the practical experiences necessary for advancement.

The exclusion from formal and informal networks of communication and control, and as a consequence, exclusion from career tracks leading to "line" (core decision-making) positions, create disadvantages that impede vertical mobility in companies. In this sense, women's particular vulnerability to power failures in management circuits brings as a corollary their over-representation in supporting function areas (such as customer relations, communications, personnel and human resources, public relations) and scarce access or exclusion from core business areas (such as marketing, finance, accounting or production).

On the assumption that social and cultural forces influence and may hinder the economic productivity of women, and that the achievement of their economic potential depends on their access to "gender-blind" career paths, managerial training, and capital and markets, the study of women and the glass ceiling in Brazil and Mexico was intended to be used towards several ends. First, it was designed to raise public awareness, mobilize political support and propose policy recommendations for an equal opportunity agenda for women in business and management. Second, the findings were to be used to propose strategies to create gender sensitivity and value diversity in management and business as a both good business practice and a way of enhancing national economies in the region.

Research and data gathering began with questionnaires addressed to CEOs, human resource directors and women in professional and managerial jobs at a selected sample of the largest companies (national, multinational and public) in the two countries as well as interviews with women business owners and with female company directors. These were supplemented by an analysis of census data and other secondary databases on employment, jobs, labour markets, business records, business directories, employers associations' directories, population and economic censuses, and ministry of labour's statistical series.

Brazil

Brazil is typical of countries in the region in that women account for an increasing number of new entrants to managerial occupations and to the business market. Women have also made great strides in education, comprising nearly 53 percent of university undergraduate and graduate enrolment, including traditional male domains such as law and business, by 1994.

Women in Management

Despite their numeric inroads into the professional ranks of management, women are still under-represented in senior executive and managerial positions, and tend to cluster in entry and middle-management positions. This seems to be true in both the private and the public sectors, although the latter is generally seen as more "open" for women's careers due to strict recruitment, promotion and pay requirements. According to 1988 Ministry of Labour figures, women directors comprised 7.3 percent in manufacturing enterprises, 7.5 percent in construction companies, and 8.3 percent in financial/ real estate/insurance companies. At the other end, women comprise 25.7 percent of intermediate administrative department heads, and 29.3 percent of intermediate department heads of accounting.

Available evidence thus shows a high percentage of women in "staff" positions, and a minority in line positions, as illustrated by women's share in the higher echelons of the corporate suite of only 3.4 percent (overall) among the top executives of the largest corporations in the country (3.7 percent in the 300 largest national private, 1.7 percent in the 20 largest state owned, and 2.6 percent in the 40 largest foreign-owned companies).[4] That ratio could have been even smaller if cases of access via kinship networks (rather than by competitive routes) had not been considered in the estimate.

As to salary, again based on 1988 figures, the ratio of female to male earnings for management jobs range from 40.8 percent in manufacturing industries, to 67.2 percent in the transport and communications sector, even though women have on average a higher educational background. In the highest salary bracket in those occupations, the ration of female to male salary can go as low as 2 percent, in the case of extractive industries and agro-industries.

The typical glass ceiling scenario was reflected in the survey responses of women professionals and managers, in terms of the factors they perceived as barriers and the actions they considered necessary to eliminate them. In addition to discrimination in hiring and promotion, they pointed to a corporate culture that devalues women; a lack of role models for women in leadership, rooted in the education system and socialization process; and the prevalence of stereotypes of women as "unfit" for business careers in business schools as well as in economics and engineering schools.

Asked what they thought should be done, the women managers stressed the need to reassess company policy and practice in recruitment, retention, and advancement of women in managerial and executive positions. They encouraged the development of support systems for balancing career and family responsibilities and an effort to value and use the talent pool represented by qualified women in the company.

Among CEOs, despite increasing discomfort about not addressing women's needs and career advancement opportunities, there were few signs of taking corporate responsibility for the inclusion of women in career planning and leadership training, tracking women with advancement potential, or introducing such innovations as flexible hours or child care in an effort to provide support for balancing career and family. Although CEOs acknowledged that stereotypes, management unwillingness to take "risks" by placing women in command positions and other gender-related preconceptions are barriers to women's access to the leadership ranks, there was little agreement about company responsibility to initiate changes to remove those barriers.

Among human resource personnel, there was limited awareness that gender-related factors might affect the success or derailment of women's careers and, further, an unwillingness to reassess company policy to provide mobility opportunities for qualified women. In general they took a "generalist" approach to human resources with little commitment to workforce diversity or equal opportunity.

Reinforcing the gender bias in corporate culture, survey responses indicated, are both executive search companies, which rely on "male"

Women managers' perceptions of barriers to career advancement

- Gender-related cultural codes
- Discriminatory practices in recruitment, promotion and development of women in professional and managerial jobs
- Lack of support systems for balancing career and family responsibilities
- Lack of opportunity for leadership training and development
- Lack of role models in executive leadership for women and lack of encouragement to assume such roles
- Self-limiting factors such as low self-esteem, low self-confidence in job performance, acceptance of lower-level jobs, fear of competition
- Woman-unfriendly corporate culture and corporate environment that stress "male" values and management styles of command
- Wide salary gaps between men and women performing managerial and executive jobs
- Prevalence of stereotypes of women as unfit for business in business schools as well as in economics and engineer-ing schools.

corporate directories and thus select women out of recruiting networks for placement in senior positions, and trade unions, which fail to include the advancement of women on the collective bargaining agenda.

Women in Business Ownership

Despite the lack of data on the demographics and performance of the female business sector (in part because internal revenue or other economic data is not analyzed or is not broken down by sex), there are indications that women have caught the entrepreneurial spirit in Brazil and are increasing their contribution to the economy, especially in the central and southern industrialized states. To discover some of the business characteristics of women-owned firms, we resorted to business directories of micro/small enterprises where women are more likely to be found. Based on a sample of 1,012 micro/small enterprises contracting SEBRAE, a semi-public support agency for small businesses, we determined that 24 percent were female headed enterprises mainly in the sectors of: fabrics and clothing (22 percent); food industry (8 percent); construction materials trade (6 percent); stationery (4 percent); and in smaller numbers in real estate, architecture and urban engineering, publicity, machines and metalwork, cosmetics, toys, leather goods, plastics, automotive retailers, security services, electrical equipment, publishing, tourism and pharmacies. They are swelling as well the ranks of entrepreneurs in franchising, as shown by a 1993 study in which 29 percent of entrepreneurs in the sample were female.[5]

But barriers to women's entrepreneurship are deeply embedded in the business world. Although the entrepreneurial culture emphasizes rationality in the mobilization of resources, problems related to sex stereotypes are frequently reported by women business owners. High transaction costs and complex application procedures limit women entrepreneurs' access to formal financial markets, making it harder for them to obtain necessary start up capital as well as funds to grow their businesses and for operational expenses. In addition, women have less access to public and private market opportunities (including procurement opportunities), technical assistance and training. Although they comprise a sizeable proportion of firms in the small-business sector, women tend to benefit less from projects designed for micro-enterprises as a result of being viewed as more prone to business failure and of being considered as a high-risk group in loan repayment.

This business environment pervades women's perceptions of barriers to entrepreneurship and of ways to remove them. Women business owners stressed the difficulties they face in getting capital at all stages of the operation; starting up, expanding, and operating. Obstacles ranged from collateral requirements for loans to stereotypes held by lending officers regarding women's ability to run their own businesses. They acknowledged a wide need for management training for women and the lack of such training or technical assistance for women interested in business careers. In addition to lending institutions, they saw women's lack of credibility among accountants and suppliers as detrimental to women's efficiency and success in business.

Women business owners indicated that a variety of resources and services were needed in order to overcome traditional sex role stereotyping and that these should be sponsored on a public/private basis. They recommended, among other things: advice on business organization and operations; reference services for the resolution of practical problems in the production of goods and services; legal advice in this regard; information about internal markets and exportation for goods and services; advice on access to capital for business financing from local sources such as state and private banks, international banks and agencies; information about franchising options; personal advice on operational questions; information about development and technology.

The women also pointed to a need to increase women's representation

Women business owners' perceptions of barriers to entrepreneurship

- Lack of management skills and lack of management and technical assistance for micro/small female-headed enterprises.
- Women's limited access to capital for starting up, expansion and operating expenses
- High costs of transactions and the complexity of requirements and procedures excluding women from formal money markets
- Collateral requirements of lending institutions
- Women's low credibility with lending institutions, and the "high risk" associated with lending to women
- Lending institutions' concerns about women's lack of technical business education and training
- Misconceptions on the part of financial institutions about women's credit-worthiness (especially with respect to loan repayment), resulting in discriminatory creditor practices
- Women's lack of credibility among accountants and suppliers

in business and employers' associations and to increase business-women's associations' influence so that women are included among the beneficiaries of public programmes and projects.

Women's Business and Professional Groups: New Developments

In 1990, women still had limited access to the major structures of corporate power and influence: women managers and entrepreneurs were either absent or had only a minority status on the boards of national and state employers associations and represented less than 3 percent on the boards of employers' unions in the country.

However, the emergence of Councils of Executive Women within the state chambers of commerce in recent years has played a significant role in mainstreaming women's interests in business, as has the proliferation of the Association of Business and Professional Women's chapters. In 1994, nine chapters of Councils of Executive Women were recorded in state capitals' chambers of commerce and in larger numbers at the municipal level. The Association of Business and Professional Women, affiliated to the International Federation of Business and Professional Women, presently has 20 chapters in state capitals and in provincial cities. A review of newsletters and reports issued by these associations indicates that they sponsor a wide range of activities and workshops, including women's empowerment initiatives, networking through professional associations, opportunities for leadership training, seminars and workshops on such issues as international trade and economic policy, relevant legislation and laws and global communications as well as technical training and financial services. Such activities suggest that in the long run, these associations may prove critical in fostering egalitarian views about men and women in the corporate world, in influencing the formation of corporate women's groups in companies, and in providing mentoring and networking opportunities as leadership training grounds for women managers and entrepreneurs.

Mexico

Research in Mexico was very difficult, owing to a general lack of availability of information and the obstacles for carrying out research on women business owners and women executives. For one thing, a lack of prior research has resulted in virtually no literature on women entrepreneurs and executives. Statistical sources presented additional problems. Most surveys and studies of companies in Mexico do not include the gender of business owners and executives in their data. In addition, statistical sources that do take gender into account, such as the National Population Census or the General Employment Surveys, do not give an altogether reliable picture. In the case of women business owners, these sources do not allow us to appraise women's participation in the informal sector of the economy or in family businesses (which are normally registered in the name of a man).

In the case of women managers, the different statistical sources are not broken down for persons earning more than ten times the minimum wage; this makes it difficult to obtain a clear estimate of managerial salaries, which on the average should be above 20 times the minimum wage and in which, due to the glass ceiling, are found the greatest differences between men and women.

In addition, we encountered a lack of cooperation in answering questionnaires. In general, people tend to be wary or simply do not have the time. Mail and fax enquiries are ignored, and information is obtained only through long insistence and through some personal calls. Following the economic crisis of December 1994, executives and officers stated that they were too overwhelmed by immediate problems to participate.

The study therefore relied on various sources, including the National Population and Housing Census for 1990 as well as former decades; the Economic Census and surveys of the status of companies in Mexico; directories of representatives and officials of companies furnished by commerce and industrial chambers and other business organizations; surveys on women entrepreneurs and women executives carried out in other countries.

We designed two questionnaires. For women entrepreneurs, a questionnaire was circulated yearly from 1991 to 1994 through the women entrepreneurs' associations. Despite their lack of statistical precision, responses allowed us to detect important trends, which were later compared to census data and other economic indicators. For the survey of women executives, a series of questionnaires was directed to general directors, human resources directors and women executives of the main companies within the Federal District in early 1995. The sample selection was taken from the directory of the country's 500 largest companies supplemented by a women's executive association's directory.

Highlights of Preliminary Findings

According to the 1990 National Census, women represent 16.32 percent of the 535,000 entrepreneurs in Mexico. A comparison of these women with the total economically active female population shows that, although women continue to be clearly in the minority, they account for 23.6 percent of the economically active population. That is, at least in the formal sector, the proportion of women business owners to all entrepreneurs is seven percentage points lower than women's representation in the economically active population, which shows that among entrepreneurs there is a greater gender-based segregation than in the economically active population as a whole.

This disparity becomes even clearer if we compare the percentage of women business owners with that of women employees and women blue-collar workers. Whereas in the blue-collar sector, for each two male workers there is one female, among employees the relationship of women to men is only one to five.

Low participation ratios are also notorious in the case of women executives. The Census indicates that of all officers and managers (569,561) in the public, private and social-welfare sectors, 81 percent are men and 19 percent are women, and at higher managerial levels there are even fewer women executives. The directory of the country's 500 largest companies lists not a single woman as a general director of a company. Among the next most senior executive positions (administrative, finance, commercial, production and human resources directors), women represent only seven percent.

In general, companies owned by women are small. Whereas, as noted, in the overall business world, the proportion of men to women is five to one, in small businesses men outnumber women by only two to one. Hence, the importance of women as small-business owners is similar to their presence as employees or blue-collar workers.

Companies owned by women are predominantly located in commercial and service sectors. In the manufacturing industry women represent only 11 percent. In activities where males predominate, such as oil and gas drilling and the construction industry, the number of women drops sharply (6.5 percent in the first case and 2.5 percent in the second). The sectors in which women business owners have the greatest presence are community and social services (39.94 percent) and the restaurant and hotel industry (33.64 percent).

Interestingly, the data suggest that women owners become integrated into managerial activities of companies as an extension of their family ties. In most cases, women business owners establish partnerships with one or more family members. The presence of women in family businesses is partially explained by the fact that they have the greatest opportunities to assume positions of authority and to work within a flexible schedule. Moreover, family businesses may provide the possibility for women to enter industries such as those of manufacturing and construction, which, as noted, have traditionally been men's fields.

For women executives in big companies, percentages depend not so much on the sector in which the company is located, but on the position women occupy within any given sector. Of a total of 194 officers holding the highest executive positions of the country's largest companies, women account for 45 percent in the human resources area; in production, by contrast, they account for only 5 percent of directive posts. It can be stated that in addition to "vertical segregation" (in which women cluster at the lower hierarchic level) there is also "horizontal segregation" (women clustering in specific fields or occupations).

Data on regional distribution confirm the link between the numerical importance of woman business owners and the size and sector of their companies. Nevertheless, women's low participation in certain states must also be explained by cultural differences and by the organizational practices of corporations. Due to certain traditional behaviour patterns that predominate among owners of large companies and members of family business groups in Nuevo Leon there is a minimal presence of both women executives and women entrepreneurs in that state.

The under-representation of women entrepreneurs in industry and their concentration in traditional commercial and services activities have been attributed to the type of interpersonal relations required in the latter activities. Women are expected to excel in these fields, due to cultural considerations as well as to the low amount of start-up capital needed in this field. In general the fact that companies owned by women are smaller than those owned by men within a given sector is partially explained by the difficulty women find in obtaining financing.

Women also tend to find barriers in family businesses, in so far as they reproduce traditional gender relations. The problems related to establishing distinctions between family and professional roles and the exercise of authority appear to be heightened by kinship and affective bonds. Similar to what occurs at home, women's work in the family business remains socially overlooked.

Within organizations, women identified cultural factors, discrimination, and Mexican "machismo" as key factors preventing them from developing and advancing. In fact, the survey shows a greater concern among women managers than among women entrepreneurs about these factors. They mention the fact that they are not taken seriously, their activities are limited, and their abilities are questioned. They note that men refuse to accept women in authority and leadership positions, making it hard for women to exercise authority and leadership. They add that men tend to exclude them from the informal circles in which much of the networking is done. These women also point to the lack of role models for women who want to combine family, career and leisure activities.

By contrast, though both women managers and women entrepreneurs find greater difficulties in obtaining training in areas such as marketing and finance, the survey showed that women entrepreneurs were more concerned about this than women executives. Perhaps, this can be explained in part by the fact that in many cases women entrepreneurs start a business with little need of a formal educational degree, while for an executive it represents a basic requirement. These women also noted the problems related to reconciling their different roles and the consequent lack of free time.

Unfortunately, and in contrast to the situation in Brazil, women are rarely found as leaders in the major business associations. In 1994, among the 75 chamber presidents that make up the Confederation of Industrial Chambers (CONCAMIN), only two women are found. In that same year, in the commercial sector, among the 304 regional chambers of commerce only 11 women were found as presidents; that is fewer than 5 percent, whereas the total number of women business owners in these fields is as high as 23 percent. The low participation of women in these organizations can also be seen in the private sector's group of advisors for the negotiations on the North American Free Trade Agreement (NAFTA) with the United States and Canada: in the case of Mexico, of the 182 business leaders there was only one woman (in the customs subgroup).

Lessons and Policy Recommendations

There seems to be a growing consensus, based on cross-national research on the fortunes and misfortunes of women in the business world, that despite expected demographic changes, time alone will not ensure women's economic power. Unless women's issues in companies are addressed as societal and organizational issues, not as individual matters, attempts to shatter glass ceilings, which block the road to women's progress, will be ineffective at best. Throughout the region, neither corporations nor governments have realized that full utilization of the talent pool represented by women is a prerequisite for achieving sustained, human-centred development and for achieving a competitive edge in the local and global marketplaces.

For this reason alone, then, governments should develop policy recommendations for an equal opportunity agenda for women in business, in management and in professional organizations, to create enforcement mechanisms and machinery for removal of barriers embedded in organizational policies and practices and in the work environment, to consider gender issues in macro-projects and policy design of development programmes, and to engage in partnership with the private sector in initiatives designed to foster women's role in professional and entrepreneurial activity, especially access to capital, markets and training. As women attain a "critical mass" in management ranks, corporate leaders must recognize their contribution to those nations' economic wealth and make the case for diversity in leadership roles so as to eliminate what was called the "sexual static" in reference to deeply rooted, subconscious discomfort at seeing females in authority roles. If this combination of normative regulation, enlightenment and demographics coalesces, it will pave the way for social change and for women's economic empowerment. ❖

---

1 UN, *1994 World Survey on the Role of Women in Development*, 1995; *The World's Women 1970-1990 - Trends and Statistics*, 1991.

2 Inter-American Development Bank, *Economic and Social Progress in Latin America - 1990 Report*, 1991.

3 US Glass-Ceiling Commission, *A Report on the Glass Ceiling Initiative*, 1991; *Good for Business*, 1995; Catalyst, *Cracking the Glass Ceiling: Strategies for Success*, 1994.

4 Balanço Anual, 1994-95, Gazeta Mercantil. Index estimates by Sonia de Avelar.

5 Index estimates by Sonia de Avelar based on SEBRAE's records; Cherto & Rizzo Franchising, *O Perfil do Franqueado Brasileiro*, 1993.

Feminism and Institutional Development: Women's NGOs in Brazil and Peru

DELAINE MARTINS COSTA AND GLEISI HEISLER NEVES*

"While changes in power relations are problematic in any organization, they are central in the case of feminist NGOs, which are themselves committed to subverting power relations in society."

NGOs in Latin America have reached a point in the process of institutional consolidation in which they must improve their administration and management capacity and attain a degree of financial autonomy, while not losing their unique nature and values. This presents a special challenge to women's NGOs, founded as they were on an awareness of the ways in which hierarchical gender relations determine the realities of women's lives and a commitment to changing the male-oriented attitudes and structures that perpetuate these relations in society. Two such feminist NGOs, both founded in the early 1980s, are the subject of this case study: Rede Mulher de Educação (Women's Education Network) in São Paulo, Brazil, and Centro Flora Tristán (Flora Tristán Centre) in Lima, Peru. While the organizational development strategies chosen by each organization were different, the process in both cases led to their growth and strengthening as agents of social change.

At the request of these organizations, UNIFEM contracted with the Brazilian Institute of Municipal Administration (IBAM), a non-profit technical-assistance organization, to engage in a process of strategic planning with both NGOs, designed to improve their administration and management structure while maintaining feminist values. The project was carried out by IBAM's Nucleus of Women's Studies and Public Policy, which was created about five years ago, primarily to help local governments incorporate a gender perspective into local policy and planning. The

---

* *Coordinated by Maria da Graca Ribeiro das Neves.*

Women's Studies Nucleus was thus in a good position not only to render strategic planning assistance to the two organizations, but also to facilitate the incorporation of a gender perspective into organizational and management theory—an additional goal of the UNIFEM project.

Beyond Power: Organizational Development in Feminist NGOs

Organizational development can be defined broadly as a process of intentional and planned change, affecting multiple aspects of the organization, from its mission, objectives, and values to its structure, work processes and members. Institutional development, on the other hand, is premised on the utilization of organizations as agents of social change, and as such necessarily goes beyond the boundaries of the organization. According to this view, institutions are organizations that can not only generate new values, attitudes, behaviour, knowledge, and technologies but also incorporate these into society. They have the capacity to win support, influence opinion, create coalitions, and progressively increase their sphere of influence. The transformation of organizations into institutions with the strength to alter or influence social relations is thus the core of institutional development.

Every process of institutional and organizational development necessarily involves a discussion about power. In the case of feminist NGOs this discussion presents a particular challenge, since these groups contest the legitimacy as well as the exercise of conventional concepts and models of power in organizations and in society.

The nineteenth-century paradigm of organization theory is the modern capitalist enterprise, the factory being its truest expression. While studies of government institutions have influenced its subsequent development, the theory is still pervaded by the dominant ideas of its time, namely positivist, market rationality and hierarchical management.

Positivism projects a concern with objectivity and neutrality, serving to cloud a variety of social norms and ideologies. These rest on a kind of rationality typical of the market that the economist Max Weber called "instrumental rationality." Instrumental rationality, unlike substantive or value rationality, is measured against calculated results or objectives. Based solely on the mechanical relation between means and ends, it does not involve a moral judgement. Substantive rationality, by contrast, has a humanistic dimension, based as it is on an ethical-normative structure. Over time, instrumental rationality became synonymous with rationality itself, with the result that almost the entire body of theory about organizations has been built around a kind of rationality that sought to enable the modern capitalist enterprise to maximize its profits (see Ramos 1981).

Recently, however, in order to respond to the demands of a rapidly changing and increasingly competitive global economy, organization theory has begun to propose more flexible and adaptable forms of organization. Changes in production as well as the gains of women and minorities in employment have brought about an appreciation of different styles of management—less hierarchical and more democratic.

One result is an effort to overcome the historic dichotomy between planning and execution, decision and action, thinking and doing, which long formed a pillar of the factory-based division of labour. Today it is clear that such separation is based on assumptions of stability that no longer hold. Rather, the behaviour of organizations is affected by several variables, many of them completely outside the organization's control. Ideas about organizations and those who work for them have become more complex and politicized, obliging the theory to deal with the problem of power.

In questioning the primacy of rationality and hierarchy in the decision-making process, students of organization theory began to pay attention to so-called female styles of management. Sylvia Vergara (1991) suggests that appreciation of a "sixth sense" is the key to opening doors for executive women, taking into consideration the argument that intuitive individuals evaluate business opportunities more easily.

Contemporary ideas about leadership and management highlight the importance and development of horizontal structures, allowing for group work, democratization of decision-making, a wider distribution of responsibilities, and more fluid information flows—all compatible with what many consider to be women's ways of managing.

In this process of theoretical revision, attributes generally regarded as female began to be considered as fundamental to their success as managers. Such theories run the risk of positing a female essence or women's "nature," employing the same stereotypes that have worked for centuries to exclude women from decision-making positions in order to argue for a "female advantage" (see Helgensen 1992; Rosener 1992). However, Heilborn and Arruda (1994) posit that by virtue of their marginalization women are not contaminated by the "dominant cultural logic" and therefore have "total understanding of and control over alternative views on how to (re)build the world". More studies on women in decision-making positions are needed to determine differences among female management styles as well as whether over time these styles differ significantly from those of men.

At the same time, if one agrees that feminism must be understood as a "set of radical ideas and practices with power to subvert, change, transform the patriarchal ideas and practices in which we live" (see Teles 1993), feminist theory must be regarded as a potential source of organizational theory revision. It is certainly true that "feminism, in its practice as a movement, has tried to overcome the traditional types of organization, permeated by asymmetry and authoritarianism" (Alves and Pitanguy 1983). In this regard, feminism offers:

- a critique of society aimed at sexual hierarchy and the sexual division of labour, rejecting the assumption that these are natural phenomena and emphasizing the fact that they are cultural constructions that can and must be changed
- a political strategy that rejects the existence of a clear limit between the private and the public spheres
- recognition of a permanent tension between the defense of equality and the recognition of difference, both between men and women and among individuals of the same sex.

The Organization of Power

Power is a focal point in organizational theory, impacting everything that refers to organizations. Yet power in organizations has not yet been sufficiently investigated, either in theory or in practice. Organization theory, by embracing the idea that organizations are rational enterprises whose members share common objectives, has ignored the political dimension of organizations. Politics is seen as a dirty word, making it difficult for those who participate in the organization to deal with this crucially important aspect of organizational reality (see Morgan 1986).

The concept of power in organizations has multiple forms, admitting different interpretations. However, it is not clear when people have power and when they exercise it as autonomous human beings; when they simply exercise power relations; whether power is a phenomenon of interpersonal behaviour or the manifestation of deeper structural factors. Most of those who study power in organizations focus on the business sector, based on instrumental rationality. For organizations guided by substantive rationality, such as NGOs, the study of power is still in its infancy.

Certainly, matters related to power require further examination, be it in the feminist debate or in organization theory. Feminist NGOs seem to be the appropriate place to put into practice the principles postulated by feminism; indeed, the hope of subverting established practices and values, especially in relation to the exercise of power, falls back upon feminist NGOs. In turn, this practice can revitalize organizational theory, by demonstrating in practice the feasibility of other forms of power. If as agents for change they are committed to transforming power relations in society, they must institutionalize appropriate power relations in their own organizations.

Feminist NGOs: The Organizational Challenge

NGOs in Latin America proliferated and grew strong in the 1970s, mainly in the context of the struggle for democracy, against authoritarianism and social injustice. In the following decades, as countries have changed, so too have NGOs themselves: many have disappeared, others have grown up, widening their mission, increasing their size and complexity, and losing their original nature as micro-organizations. At the same time, however, economic constraints have made the financial survival of most NGOs in the region increasingly problematic. NGOs on the one hand have never had their importance so widely recognized, both nationally and internationally; on the other hand, they are experiencing a unprecedented financing crisis, which affects their performance and even their survival.

As a result, NGOs throughout the region are confronting a need to recognize their growing pains and the implications for restructuring.
NGOs in Latin America, as elsewhere, often owe their creation to the leadership capacity of one of its members. However, leadership alone is not enough; managerial abilities have to be developed. This is the opposite of what occurs in large corporations where the main challenge today is to transform managers into leaders. Leadership capacity must be added to managerial capacity—one has to be acquired without losing the other. Thus, NGO leaders have to prepare themselves to operate in the managerial dimension.

Usually, NGOs are created out of loyalty to a subject and a task—feminism and popular education, for instance. But at some point it becomes necessary to change this loyalty into loyalty to the organization itself, which otherwise cannot survive. Thus, an interdependence arises between the defense of the subject, the success of the task, and the survival of the organization. In the case of feminist NGOs, an effort is added to avoid reproducing hierarchical patterns predominant in patriarchal society, thus looking for organizational forms that value symmetry in power relations.

The feeling of belonging to the organization is given, at the beginning, by the involvement with subject and task. Then, professionalism develops not only because of affinity with the subject but also because of self-interest, search for prestige, and convenience. In building a career in a feminist NGO the demands of a work day go beyond the organization. They may overburden women, fostering tensions in the very fields where feminist NGOS perform, such as women's double role.

A problem occurs when NGOs switch from an organization of peers to an employee-employer relation organization. In feminist NGOs these characteristics may become more acute due to the principle of radical democracy and to the fact that they are organizations of women for women; that is, self-referred. They tend to value "symbolic adherence" rather than material benefits as sources of motivation and also value dedication to the "cause" over specific competence for the exercise of functions. Since efficiency is not their main concern, they face serious financial limitations to improve their wage policy.

Many NGOs develop around specific projects formulated and managed with a high level of autonomy, creating a dilemma between a visionary style of management and the pragmatism inherent in a project-based organization. Planning must therefore incorporate a holistic view of the organization and incorporate all levels. It must also be directly associated to management—strategic planning and strategic management are increasingly considered part of the same process.

In a context of so many changes, the survival of NGOs, in Latin America as elsewhere, seems to depend on their capacity to face new challenges and dilemmas. NGOs tend to live the tension between the new professionalism, typical of what in organization theory is called instrumental rationality, and the feminist values already incorporated into their organizational culture. In some cases, resistance and even rejection of the former are frequent. In other cases, if NGOs place their own survival above all, adherence to professionalism can mean becoming bureaucratic, risking their objectives, identity and legitimacy.

No change in an organization is neutral, since changes necessarily involve matters related to power. The problem for NGOs, especially feminist NGOs, is to decide how to structure themselves without betraying their convictions.

Two Feminist NGOs

The Women's Education Network (Rede Mulher de Educacão) in São Paulo is committed to feminist popular education. Founded in 1984, it defines its mission as: *improving gender relations through feminist popular education, understood as a pedagogical and political process aimed at reciprocity between men and women in all spheres of life.*

Like many organizations that started in the late 1970s and early 1980s, the Women's Education Network has experienced a quantum leap in its influence and activities. Starting with a recognition of the need to draw attention to women's needs, including their right to use their own bodies, the organization began to use popular education to address the demands of the many women that made up its network—then organized loosely in various church groups, political parties, or charity organizations and for the most part totally dependent on these different organizations. The network has expanded exponentially from its base in the outskirts of Sao Paulo, and currently coordinates the political activities of over 3,000 women in 700 groups, ranging from poor women in local parishes to educated professional women. The organization publishes a newsletter and houses a documentation centre, where it distributes books, magazines and tapes. It also sponsors frequent workshops, designed to bring together women in various walks of life from all over the country.

The Flora Tristán Centre in Lima was created in 1979. So closely is it linked to the women's movement in Peru that in its early years it was difficult to distinguish between the two. While the line had become clearer by 1982, their close interaction has endured. Over the years, moreover, the Centre has strengthened its ties with the different tendencies of the women's movement.

Responding to the impact of globalization and the declining power of the state, the Flora Tristán Centre is seeking to insert a gender perspective into the subsequent redefinition of relations between society and the state. It has set the following institutional goal for the next five years: *to influence not only the areas where opinions are generated and policies formulated concerning central aspects of women's lives, but also the individual and collective processes necessary to achieve women's emancipation and gender-*

related justice. The organization has developed a variety of projects designed to improve the quality of women's lives, many in collaboration with other coalitions, such as the Women's Forum, which focuses on legislation in favour of women, and the National Network for Women's Advancement. The Centre is concerned to make its work known nationwide; it has a vast communication programme and an excellent reputation. It has also been actively engaged in several United Nations conferences, both as an NGO and as part of the government delegation.

The process of strategic planning at both organizations was assisted by a number of agencies, including the Women's Institute of the Ministry of Social Affairs in Spain and the United Nations Development Programme's Management and Development Programme, a collaboration that was beneficial to all of the organizations involved.

IBAM's role was to enable the organizations to identify the main organizational problems, indicating alternative ways to face or solve them, with the advantages and disadvantages of each. The intention was to act as a catalyst, helping the organizations to think critically about their own problems and find solutions to them. The first, and ongoing, step in this process was the identification of the difficulties faced by each organization based on the perception of their own members, in the belief that dissatisfaction contains a great potential for change. The critical capacity and creativity brought by these organizations were decisive factors in the success of the undertaking.

Women's Education Network

From the outset it was clear that the Women's Education Network viewed the preparation of new bylaws as crucial. Because the organization was undergoing a period of transition and change, the results of which should be reflected in the by-laws, members thought the project should provide the vehicle through which to draw these up. Changes had to do with the leave of absence of the organization's founder and director as well as the need to develop the organization as a network.

The focus on by-laws resulted from a previous evaluation exercise, in which problems ranging from staff dissatisfaction to lack of clarity about goals and objectives had been perceived as resulting from outdated and inappropriate by-laws. IBAM argued that new by-laws should be the outcome of a process of reflection, analysis and discussion; the formalization of a planned change. At times this was a source of tension, since often the very issue the organization wanted to be solved as quickly as possible—and for that purpose was counting on IBAM's support—was instead treated as a problem to be discussed. IBAM considered that the lack of discussion was part of the overall organizational problem and that it should try to bring these needs to light, allowing the organization to develop its own mechanisms to deal with the problems it was undergoing.

Strategic planning

The first step in the process of strategic planning involved a workshop, drawing on participatory methodology that allowed for the best possible contribution of group members. Given the organization's goal of achieving a better balance between its organizational requirements and its relations and functions as a network, the workshop concentrated on this task. To facilitate the discussion the term "tear" (loom) was proposed for the non-profit organization, and "trama" (weft) for the network of relations. The workshop was responsible for clarifying the purpose and function of each as well as pointing out new issues in order to make the organization's work more consistent. The workshop enabled participants to carefully discuss the following:

- the mission of the organization
- organizational structure (main decision-making levels and role of affiliates)
- strategic lines of action, considering both opportunities and constraints to develop its mission.

A consensus emerged that the organization should improve strategies to weave its own organizational weft in order to establish its own limits, possibilities and needs to operate as a centre or network. It is worth remembering the phrase used by members of the organization referring to the need to make the actual existence of the NGO compatible with its desire to become a service network: "an NGO in its institutionality, and a network in its functionality." The organization now has a much more holistic view of its future, and it is in a better position to make further changes in its by-laws.

New by-laws

The main points covered by the new by-laws include:

- **identification of the feminist nature of the organization**—a new feature for by-laws in general, and for the by-laws of the Women's Education Network in particular, giving more visibility to the identity of the organization.
- **definition of its basic principles**—to include, among others, women's rights as human rights, gender-related social relations, popular education and women's self-organization.
- **maintenance of an "Escola de Formação" (School of Education), and creation of a service network to support women's self-organization.**
- **definition of membership categories** in line with the mission and objectives of the organization, to include: a) honorary members, b) *sócias educadoras* (members devoted to popular education), and c) affiliate members, specifying their rights and obligations.
- **changes in decision-making** to incorporate a "Colegiado de Direção Executiva," an executive board whose members have identical powers. This is comprised of the programme coordinators of the School of Education and is responsible for the management and implementation of the organization's activities. The former by-laws did not address management structure, leaving this to the organization itself, thus risking the development of a concentrated, centralized, and hierarchical decision-making process. The creation of the colegiado and its incorporation into the by-laws not only facilitates more horizontal power relations, but also guarantees structural continuity.

While organizational by-laws are legally required in Brazil, often they are a formality only, establishing *pro forma* rules. This was certainly the case with the Women's Education Network, which to comply with the law, simply copied the by-laws from another organization. Ten years later, the organization found itself with a set of by-laws that were useless in terms of being able to guide and give norms for the functioning of the organization.

The new by-laws reflect an organizational model in which power is structured horizontally—the *colegiado* (a shared decision board) being an example—and are therefore more consistent with the original feminist purposes. They reflect the effort to incorporate the central values of feminism (e.g., equality, freedom, autonomy, democracy) into the organizational structure.

Preparation of internal rules and rules of personnel

In accordance with the changed by-laws, the organization requested IBAM to assist in drawing up internal rules for the School of Education—including the functions of the organization, its compensation and career development plans, administrative structure, and so on. The rules represent an attempt to resolve a number of organizational problems, such as work flow; lack of criteria by which to respond to external demands; devotion to militancy with no priorities for action; the invisibility of women's work, obscuring both that which is being done well and those who are not doing their part within the organization; tension concerning the decision-making process and possible hierarchies resulting from it; increasing demand for professionalization; and women's domestic responsibilities and implications for workplace relations.

In drawing up organizational rules, it is important to consider uses and "disuses" of the rules, especially for NGOs that tend to value informality, activism and participation in the decision-making process. While there is no need to disregard or even change these values, it is necessary to clarify them, making the dynamics of the organization clear for those who are part or will become part of it. In this regard, it is also important to distinguish formal rules or procedures—including criteria for recruiting and selection of personnel, compensation and career development opportunities—from the informal ones that permeate the organization. Standardization of work practices is designed to separate formal lines of authority from informal lines of power, in order to facilitate more symmetrical relations within the workplace and allow greater horizontalization of power (see Pages 1993).

Flora Tristán Centre

In the project with Flora Tristán, IBAM identified three relevant points: 1) the Centre operated as a collective prior to becoming an NGO; 2) a large number of reports had been produced as a result of external technical assistance and evaluation carried out by financing agencies; and 3) a recent strategic planning process had yielded a sectional view of the organization rather than a view of it as a whole.

The first site visit therefore was designed to obtain a more holistic view of the organization, in order to avoid duplicating the previous planning exercise as well as to better incorporate its feminist values, including participation, dialogue, and so on. The resulting diagnosis included the following needs:

- **attention to the organizational culture.** Working with the organizational culture was essential in order to reconcile both 1) the organizational values linked to feminism with the need to increase administrative efficiency and 2) the organization's past with its future.
- **alterations in the organizational structure.** Structural changes were needed to clarify the division of tasks and distribution of authority and decision-making responsibility within the organization as well as to specify the functions of the several organizational levels, units and work groups. These changes should facilitate internal integration, improve communication and information flows, and avoid duplication of effort and resources—and thereby achieve more professional management without generating bureaucratic, centralized, authoritarian, hierarchical and "heavy" structures.
- **creation of new "organizational spaces and mechanisms."** The need for new avenues for discussion of ideas, exchange of knowledge and experiences, and socialization of new employees sprang both from the need of all organizations to invest in staff development and from the centre's need to clarify the linkage between its mission and its various programmes.
- **internalization of strategic planning, management and project evaluation.** In order to enhance the organization's role as agent of social change it was necessary to avoid fragmentation of programmes and projects, and endeavour to institutionalize planning as an ongoing process. It was emphasized that the planning process should start from a holistic view of the institution,

linking a strategic view of planning to a strategic view of management.

- **definition of human resources policy.** The need to clearly define a human resources policy, mainly regarding compensation and career development, was an urgent staff priority, as was the preparation of a job reclassification plan and a manual for job classification and career development.
- **establishment of rules for organizational functioning and interpersonal interaction.** Although the absence of clear rules and procedures had resulted in the perception of administrative disorder and interpersonal injustice, any effort to establish such rules had to overcome resistance springing from the failure of previous attempts to establish rights and obligations and the belief that such procedures were somehow in conflict with feminist values.

Since the initial request for technical assistance stressed administration as the main problem, it was possible to widen the scope of the discussion by relating organizational development to institutional development. It became clear that in order to enhance the capacity of the centre as an agent of social change, priority should be given to strategic planning and administrative restructuring, with additional areas scheduled for future attention.

The organization instituted a number of structural changes, culminating in the General Assembly in December 1994, when strategic lines of action and a new administrative structure were approved. Among the main changes were the creation of a Directorio, or shared-administration board, the position of Executive Director, and Functional Managerial Units, which combine functional and subject areas in a matrix structure.

A second process of strategic planning, based on the restructuring proposal approved by the General Assembly, was then undertaken. This began by defining some of the terms of strategic planning as well as clarifying the responsibilities of units and individuals in order to fix more clearly the limits of the managerial areas and strategic lines of action. The project produced the following strategic lines of action:

- creating a unit to give technical support and assistance to institutional development and organizational change, especially the process of strategic planning. IBAM considered this unit essential to long-term improvement;

• redefining the concept of projects and highlighting their importance for micro-planning. A project should be understood as the basic element of job organization, management and implementation, since it can confer flexibility and agility to the organization.

Concluding Observations

The observations that follow are intended for reflection in carrying out similar experiments in other organizations. More generally, they should provoke more penetrating reflections about organizational development in NGOs, especially those based on feminist values and experience.

The challenge of translating feminist principles into organizational practice is considerable. There are very few studies about organizations that take gender relations into consideration or that use gender as a category of analysis, and those that do exist are not readily available. Reflecting the gulf between gender and organizational theory, it was difficult to find professionals in administration who were familiar with gender studies. Thus, the project had to rely on people in different fields who accepted the challenge of reflecting, together with the organizations involved, about gender, NGOs and organizational theory. Moreover, in view of the fact that NGO members were both subject and object of their own reflections, the organization in which they work formed a pervasive context: it is the space where subjectivity, knowledge and the discourse about gender and feminism are produced. On the other hand, in this same space are created the relations that should be coherent with this discourse. While changes in power relations are problematic in any organization, they are central in the case of feminist NGOs, which are themselves committed to subverting power relations in society.

Studies of women's leadership and management frequently tend to reject one set of stereotypes by using another set of stereotypes. Such studies often overestimate so-called female qualities or traits, bestowing on them an advantage rather than a disadvantage for women in the organization. Few such studies are conducted in the non-profit sector, and fewer still are based on women's organizations. If one agrees that a primary objective of feminist theory is "to analyze how we think, or do not think, or avoid thinking about gender" (see Flax 1991), organizational theory must be seen as a stimulating and poorly explored field for this analysis.

While the development strategies chosen by the Women's Education Network and the Flora Tristán Centre were different, the process of organizational change in both cases has led to the enlargement and strengthening of the NGOs as agents of social change. Both showed a capacity for radical restructuring, in contrast to the incremental changes normally adopted by public sector organizations, which were attributed to their willingness to deal with conflict. Both NGOs shared a strong preference for participatory, flexible and open administrative and managerial structures rather than hierarchical or formalist models of power. Thus, the touchstone of the new management strategies is the commitment to a progressive set of ideas and objectives permeated by feminism (see Heilborn and Arruda 1994).

At different phases of the project both NGOs showed some reluctance to adopt concepts and methodologies widely accepted within organizational theory. This is probably due to the influence of feminist thinking, which is suspicious of knowledge built up by a patriarchal society and under the dominance of instrumental rationality.

While the skepticism is justified, given the bias of organizational theory, it may also be true that such skepticism can induce some organizations to rely only on their own experience, obliging them to constantly need to "re-invent the wheel," that is, to develop their own concepts and methodologies instead of criticizing and adapting existing ones. Another issue is to find out to which extent reliance on purely feminist "language" hinders communication, for instance, with the state, international agencies or other organizations.

NGOs' ability to value strategic planning and be able to employ it in a concrete situation can help avoid a number of problems common to NGOs, including

- dependence on "charismatic leadership"
- appraisals with no clear parameters of reference and no clear analytical justification
- unsystematic managerial procedures
- difficulties in fundraising, arising from a lack of systematic reflection about strategies
- weak formulation of programmes and projects of the organization.

In order to become self-sustaining, NGOs such as the Women's Education Network and the Flora Tristán Centre must resolve the dilemma between adhering to the original mission and adopting more professional managerial practices. The incorporation of more managerial practices will tend to change organizational management style, giving greater importance to issues such as financial efficiency, profitability and productivity; setting of priorities to attend demands; more formal rules for organizational functioning and interpersonal interaction as well as work processes, power structures and responsibilities of units and individuals. None of these require a radical change of perspective; adopting managerial logic is possible without breaking with the mission, the system of values, and the very philosophy of the organization.

The challenge, in short, is that of reconciling the past with the future, keeping the balance between efficiency and effectiveness. In this sense, it is necessary to overcome the tendency, common in NGOs, to find in their past an excuse for their problems, and overestimate the importance of historic coherence and loyalty to their origins.

In the course of strategic planning and administrative restructuring, both organizations raised issues of financial autonomy in a search for self-sustainability and in an effort to improve financial management efficiency. The groups took different routes in their search for self-sustainability. The Women's Education Network intends to invest in for-profit events in order to raise money for those non-profitable activities related to its mission. However, it does not want to directly intervene in the management of these events, since it recognizes that they require a different logic and procedures. By contrast, Flora Tristán was seeking to increase traditional sources of financing (e.g., publications, selling of information), while studying the possibility of obtaining financial support from its beneficiaries — launching an insurance programme for women against violence, for instance. Its strategy seems to be to increase revenue through activities compatible with the development of its mission, but from a gender perspective.

Both NGOs have a consensus about the need for greater professionalization. Thus, the importance of human resources training as well as permanent job retraining was stressed often, as was the possibility of hiring specialists for certain managerial jobs. The Flora Tristán Centre, for example, has considered hiring an administrative and financial professional manager to oversee administration and train employees in this area. However, the idea that such a manager requires specific technical training, not merely leadership ability, was not fully appreciated. One of the issues that both organizations must face is that of militancy versus professionalism.

Both the Women's Education Network and the Flora Tristán Centre now have a more integrated perception of themselves and a clearer view of their identity, mission, and future. But planning is an ongoing process in which new issues arise, perceptions, decisions and previous practices are re-examined, courses of action are corrected. Although the value of planning as a permanent process has been recognized, its de facto internalization and day-to-day operation will not be easy.

In terms of administrative restructuring, while both NGOs have chosen to formalize the distribution of power and responsibilities, they have avoided the pitfalls of the bureaucratic model—that is, excessive centralization, verticalization, and departmentalization—adopting a network or matrix structure that contributes to organizational flexibility, integration, cooperation, creativity and innovation. The shared-administration boards created by both NGOs reflect a concern to reconcile more efficient decision-making without giving up democratic participation. However, it is important to note that these structural forms do not lead necessarily to the solution of problems related to the exercise of power in organizations.

Finally, are there general lessons for NGOs who seek to increase their efficiency without losing sight of their humanistic and emancipation values and objectives? Is it inevitable that these objectives reproduce the logic of domination and oppression that characterize work relations?

Such questions address the problem of reconciling two ways of thinking, instrumental and substantive rationality, the first of which has long dominated the second. One possibility is the adoption of communicative rationality, a concept proposed by the sociologist Jurgen Habermas: "not an abstract faculty, inherent to the isolated individual, but an argumentative procedure through which two or more individuals agree about truth, justice, and authenticity..." (see Freddo 1991). Proponents believe that through this new kind of rationality individuals can recognize, anticipate, and oppose themselves to procedures that generate distortions in communication and serve to reproduce relations of domination and oppression within organizations.

Whatever the resolution for organizational theory, feminist NGOs offer a fertile field for theoretical reflection and experience. They can also facilitate for the criticism of the economic paradigm underlying the organizational theory or promote the search for an antiparadigm.

It is necessary that gender be used as a category of analysis in organizational theory studies, especially with regard to management, in order to enlarge this debate, making it more consistent and critical. It is also important that gender-related studies or those which incorporate these categories be in constant contact with the insights of feminist theory. Finally, it is necessary to broaden the discussion about the influence of feminism on women's NGOs. The incorporation of gender issues by NGOs in general and by those devoted exclusively to this subject deserves to be investigated in order to better understand the activities of the NGO sector and its impact on the female condition. ❖

References

ALVES, Branca Moreira, and PITANGUY, Jacqueline. *O que é feminismo.* 3rd edition. São Paulo: Brasiliense, 1983.

FLAX, Jane. Pós-modernismo e relações de gênero na teoria feminista. In: HOLANDA, Heloísa Buarque de (org.). *Pós-modernismo e política.* Rio de Janeiro, Rocco, 1991, pp. 217-249.

FREDDO, Antonio Carlos. O discurso gerencial como lógica da dominação na organização. *Revista de Administração Pública,* Rio de Janeiro, vol. 25, no. 2, pp. 73-85, Apr.-Jun. 1991.

GUERREIRO RAMOS, Alberto. *A nova ciência das organizações: uma reconceituação da riqueza das nações.* Rio de Janeiro: FGV, 1981.

HEILBORN, Ma. Luiza, and ARRUDA, Angela. "Legado feminista e ONGs de mulheres: notas preliminares." Paper presented at the seminar Strategic Planning and Organizational Development under a Gender Perspective, São Paulo, 23-27 March 1994. Rio de Janeiro: IBAM/ENSUR/NMPP, 1994.

________ . "Relações de gênero e desenvolvimento institucional: dilemas e desafios enfrentados por ONGs na América Latina." Rio de Janeiro: n.p. 1994.

HELGESEN, Sally. *La ventaja femenina: como dirigen las mujeres.* Madrid, Instituto de la Mujer, 1992.

PAGÈS, Max et al. *O poder das organizações.* São Paulo: Atlas, 1993.

ROSENER, Judy. *El estilo de dirección femenino.* Madrid: Instituto de la Mujer, 1992. (Resúmenes de textos sobre gestión directiva, A 2.92).

TELES, Ma. Amélia de Almeida. *Breve história do feminismo no Brasil.* São Paulo: Brasiliense, 1993.

VERGARA, Sylvia Constant. Razão e intuição na tomada de decisão: uma abordagem exploratória. *Revista de Administração Pública,* vol. 25, no. 3, pp. 120-138, Jul.-Sep.1991.

Paying Our Way: A Women's Fund in Mexico

LUCERO GONZALEZ AND JOANNE SANDLER

"Instead of regarding giving as a social obligation, people should think in terms of building partnerships to support the many groups in the country that promoted women's leadership in collective efforts to seek solutions to entrenched problems.."

Only 25 years ago, the idea of finding full-time, paid employment doing feminist organizing was an unheard of notion. Volunteer work could be found and it was not unusual for women to have full-time "mainstream" jobs and hold an essentially second full-time vocation that involved feminist organizing in the evenings and on weekends. But the idea of a feminist "career" was a dream. The triple day—one's paid employment, housework, and women's movement work—seemed an inevitability.

During the 1970s and 1980s, this situation changed in almost every continent of the world. Women built organizations and raised money so that staff could be hired and a longer-term commitment to working on projects and initiatives could be secured. The world attention that focused on women and women's organizations as a result of the UN Decade for Women (1975-1985), the bilateral agency financing and consequent government support that became available as a result, as well as the recognition that national development was linked to women's advancement, created "career tracks" for women who were committed to working for women's rights, their economic security and social transformation.

By the early 1980s, the numbers of women's organizations around the world that were grappling with structural issues of survival, power and growth swelled. No longer were we raising money just to support projects and financing the infrastructure by doing work out of our homes and in our off hours. Our organizations were institutionalizing and, as a result, the funds that we raised were also needed to support office space, electricity, social security and health insurance for staff, and salaries. We struggled with questions that burgeoning institutions must confront: What was the value of our time and skills, both in the marketplace and in relation to each other? How much of our autonomy could be bargained for a needed grant? How could we make long-term commitments to our project partners and staff when our survival was based on the priorities and board decisions of foundations and government agencies?

Tina Johnson of the Caribbean Association for Feminist Research and Action (CAFRA) addressed some of these questions. In a 1990 article she wrote: "One issue [for us] is the question of 'self-sufficiency.' It is not only a demand from the funders. There is a concern about whether we want to be totally dependent on funding agencies, especially as they begin to shift their money into other areas. At CAFRA, we have always argued that it is impossible for a membership network which runs projects in different territories to be totally self-sufficient." Speaking of her work in a rape crisis centre, she added: "There is no way to organize rape survivors into some income generating project to support rape crisis centres." Instead, she said, "There is a need for NGOs in the Caribbean to get together to meet with funding agencies so that rather than funding agencies telling us what our priorities should be...we can be telling them what our needs are."

As women confronted these and other issues, it became clear that we needed new sources of funding and new institutions to provide these resources. There was an urgent need for support for "risky" projects (e.g., those dealing with emerging issues for women, start-up organizations, or those involved in controversial initiatives) and for investments made to build feminist leadership and feminist institutions. There was also an interest in developing innovative approaches to funding. What would happen if, for instance, grantees were involved in the grantmaking process? What if the boards of directors and staff of grantmaking organizations included women from the communities that were being assisted?

The need for more flexible and accessible sources of funding led to the creation of women's funds. In the 1970s, a number of North American and European women began to form small funds for women. One of the first such funds was the Ms. Foundation for Women, which began in New York City in 1972. In subsequent years funds for women proliferated throughout states and localities; today there are over 70 such funds in the United States. The women's funds organize and meet annually as part of a national network of women's funds, and while many of them continue to struggle to achieve financial security, it is estimated that in 1992 they raised over $17.4 million and dispensed $9 million in grants.

Women's funds offer a lifeline to many struggling grassroots organizations and provide technical assistance and support for other funding strategies.[1] Most of these funds were established to support women in a small geographic area. Most, as well, were started with the idea of raising money from a source that women's organizations traditionally found difficult to reach: individuals. Individuals are a critical source of funds for all non-profit endeavours: in the United States, more than 80 percent of all charitable giving each year now comes from living individuals, with only about 13 percent coming from foundations and corporations.

While in the United States, the women's funding network began with a strong focus on funding locally, there was a slower but noticeable increase, as well, in women's funds that worked internationally. The United Nations Development Fund for Women (UNIFEM) became the first autonomous women's fund in the United Nations system in 1976 and was established to support women's economic empowerment. Mama Cash in the Netherlands and MATCH in Canada also formed in the 1970s to provide seed money to women's projects. In the 1980s, the Global Fund for Women in California was established as an autonomous women's funding agency to support projects in the Third World. These, and the other women's Funds that have emerged in the North, have built close ties with sisters in the Third World and have been at the forefront of creating North/South partnerships based on equity and exchange of skills and know-how.

By the late 1980s, in part as a result of their close ties to women's funding networks in the North, women in the South became increasingly interested in establishing similar organizations in their own countries. The prospect was a challenging one. First, the philanthropic tradition is different. While in the North there are tax incentives to encourage donations to non-profits, from individuals as well as foundations, these incentives are generally absent in countries of the South. Perhaps more important, the large middle class, which provides the primary source of money in response to popular campaigns on social issues in the North, is only nascent or even absent in the South. Finally, the numbers of very wealthy individuals, who can be asked for thousands of dollars in the form of a gift or an endowment, are much smaller in the Third World than in the North.

Nevertheless, in the early 1990s, women in a number of countries in the South, including the Philippines, Zimbabwe and Mexico, began to organize to set up autonomous women's funds. The Global Fund for Women has been a significant partner in several of these start-ups and has provided financial and technical support to groups interested in creating women's funds in these countries.

One of the first groups to launch a women's fund in the Third World was the Mexican Society for Women's Rights (Sociedad Mexicana pro Derechos de la Mujer) in Mexico City. With a small seed grant from the Global Fund for Women, the Sociedad was formed in 1990 with the aim of raising funds to support women's projects throughout the country. The challenge for the organization was to identify sources of financing that were currently unavailable to women's groups and to expand public interest and support for women's organizing activities.

Shaping a philanthropic organization to support women

The Sociedad began with the idea of inspiring a new tradition in philanthropy. In Mexico, philanthropy has always been linked to charity and the church, based around the conception of giving to the poor. The organization's founders hoped they could transform people's thinking about philanthropy: instead of regarding giving as a social obligation, people should think in terms of building partnerships to support the many groups in the country that promoted women's leadership in collective efforts to seek solutions to entrenched problems. The goal was to build bridges between the world of finance and donors — both men and women — and the web of organizations that women were creating. Through this, they hoped to promote a recognition that organizing for social change could be enhanced through a collective effort between donors, groups of women and the community.

As the organization grew, it went through two phases. In the first phase, from 1990 to 1993, organizers brought together women from different disciplines to learn about philanthropy in the non-profit world and to promote citizen participation. Funding during the first three years, came primarily from international foundations in the United States, including the John D. and Catherine T. MacArthur Foundation, the Ford Foundation, the Global Fund for Women, as well as international agencies such as UNIFEM. Some of the money that came from these sources was to support the Sociedad's institution-building efforts, such as hiring core staff, doing outreach to its constituency and developing a strategic plan to identify new sources of funding for women's organizations. But, the majority went directly to support proposals selected by the organization's board of directors.

During the first three years, 23 women's groups received financing. Funds were allocated to three types of projects: women's rights as human rights, economic self-sufficiency for women, and media and communications projects designed to raise consciousness about women's issues and projects organized to address them. Organizations also had to meet certain criteria: they had to be committed to advancing women's rights and participation, and they had to demonstrate that they had the capacity to follow up after their seed money ran out or that they had a longer-term plan. The projects supported during this first phase were varied: women's radio programmes in Oaxaca, a group of community organizers working on public education campaigns to stop violence against women in San Luis Potosí, and projects on the U.S.-Mexican border to educate women in the maquila about workers' and health rights.

It was during this first phase of the organization's existence that its staff and board realized that the seed money they had to invest in women's projects fell far short of the need. They received many proposals that were slightly outside of their guidelines but which were important efforts. They also received proposals within their guidelines that they simply lacked funds to support. With a commitment to build the growing strength of a network of women's organizations, the Sociedad took, as part of its mission, the mandate of helping women's groups to identify sources of funding, even when their requests did not fit the organization's guidelines.

Building women's capacity to raise money

After participating in a fundraising training workshop sponsored by the Colegio de Mexico and the International Women's Tribune Centre in 1991, the founders of the Sociedad for Women's Rights decided to develop a workshop series designed to teach women's groups throughout the country to craft proposals and identify sources of funding. Participants in these workshops would include groups that the organization had supported, as well as those that had never applied. The objective was to build the capacity of the groups with which it was partnering so that the organization could continue to spread seed money to new groups while the groups that it had supported initially could graduate to larger and more established sources of support.

The organization's staff designed a three-day workshop that built practical skills in proposal writing and asking for money, involved groups in researching and sharing information about funding sources, and also provided opportunities to discuss the complexities of donor-grantee relationships, participants' attitudes about money and power, and longer-term issues related to building sustainable organizations.

In 1992, UNIFEM gave the organization a small grant to organize five workshops. Over a period of five months, the workshops were held in Chiapas, Oaxaca, San Luis Potosí, Tijuana and Cuernavaca. In total, 53 groups participated. True to its values, the Sociedad organized these workshops by developing a series of partnerships. A local group in each city was responsible for deciding who should be invited, arranging for a workshop space and managing the logistics. It was also required to convene follow-up meetings with the groups that attended, in order to continue the focus on securing financing, as well as to make a commitment to replicate the workshop at least once. The workshops thus became a positive impetus for building collaboration among women's groups in each city.

The workshop design was participatory, interactive, and based on non-formal education principles. During the first day of the workshop, participants assessed their own attitudes towards asking for money and identified their strengths and weaknesses in the various tasks associated with fundraising. Not surprisingly, for many women in the room the least desirable aspect of fundraising was going to donors and asking for money. Participants talked about their discomfort in asking for money, their fear of hearing "no," and the fact that they were trained to do community work, not to become professional fundraisers. Many participants, however, could identify fundraising-related tasks that they did enjoy: proposal writing, research, giving feedback to peers and others.

The first day also included activities that helped participants to see fundraising as a strategic and ongoing process that was rooted in relationship-building. Facilitators used examples and mini-case studies to demonstrate that the hundreds of hours that groups frequently invest in writing and fielding unsolicited proposals needs to be balanced with (and frequently preceded by) making contacts in the donor world and building partnerships with donor agencies. All of these activities were designed to help participants understand the many tasks and skills involved in generating organizational resources and to see that, whatever their likes and dislikes, they could play important roles in contributing to strategies and campaigns to increase organizational resources. They were also designed to provoke wide-ranging discussions about the intricacies of donor-grantee relationships and the power and self-sufficiency issues that emerge as groups become more dependent on outside funding.

During the second day, the group concentrated on project proposals, learning the essential elements of proposal writing, critiquing examples of good and inadequate proposals and sharing their own project proposals with colleagues to receive feedback and ideas. Workshop facilitators reviewed a variety of donor-agency proposal-format requirements and discussed ways of streamlining the proposal-writing process. Peer critique on this day helped participants to understand and avoid the tendency to draft a proposal in which 75 percent of the text reported on the organization's research into a problem and only a small part of the proposal discussed what the organization was planning to do about it. Discussion also focused on the importance of calculating and including accurate and detailed budgets that were consistent with the project activities described. In this session, participants talked a great deal about the difficulty that they had in valuing their own time and their tendency to rely on volunteer work. In the final session of the day participants began to create their own fundraising directories, sharing information about the sources of support they had secured and the strategies that they felt were most effective in inspiring donor confidence.

The final day of the workshop was designed around role plays, involving participants in presenting their proposal ideas to representatives of donor agencies who agreed to participate. Field staff from UNIFEM's Mexico office cooperated in these role plays and offered useful feedback to participants on different ways of presenting ideas and expanding their contacts. In the final session, participants created action plans and commitments to continue to check in with their colleagues about their progress in fundraising.

Each workshop included a significant period, at the end, for on-site evaluation of the process. At each site, participants commented on the usefulness of the content and the approach. A frequent comment was that the workshop helped them to see the value of sharing information of this type. Many had come to the workshop believing that knowledge about a potential source of programme funding was to be guarded. The workshop helped them to understand that, while sharing this information might increase demand on donors, this demand could be an impetus for donors to increase, rather than decrease, their funds to women's initiatives. Particularly relevant was the experience of projects to end violence against women. Participants could all cite examples of the way in which, in the 1980s, bilateral and multilateral donors did not see violence against women as a development issue. But as the international networks focusing on violence against women grew, as local level work on the issue garnered public attention, and as more groups sprouted up around the world, bilateral and multilateral donors began receiving more proposals requesting funds for battered women's shelters, anti-violence campaigns, and other human rights-related work. The pressure of demand created new funds in donor agencies that could be channeled to this work.

Reflecting on the process

The groups that participated in the 1992 workshop series fulfilled their commitment to replicate the training. In some cases, such as in Tijuana, organizers used the Sociedad's materials to hold additional workshops. In other places, the follow-up was different. In Oaxaca, the groups decided that rather than replicate the workshop, they would find it more useful to begin a process of continuous sharing of information, both in written form and through organizing meetings to talk about fundraising.

Lucero Gonzalez, director of the Sociedad at the time of the workshops, offered several reflections on the process:

> Through the workshops, we helped women to understand that money is accessible and that there are steps and processes for gaining access. In the process of talking about the need for money and ways of securing it, the groups inevitably affirmed their own efforts and took a closer look at the necessity of creating places for women to work, where they are remunerated fairly and have a longer-term sense of job security. Actually, an important theme of the workshop was that of valuing our work. This is not just in relation to the fact that women need to be paid, but also in terms of the donor/grantee relationship. The workshops helped us to develop a better definition of this relationship and helped participants to see that they were bringing the value of their community initiatives to the table, which was equal in value to the money that the donors were giving. This helped groups to approach negotiations with

donors agencies and institutions with greater strength and confidence.

The workshops were also a place to talk about relationship-building and longer-term organizational sustainability. Many groups did not recognize the importance of maintaining contact with donors after a grant had been received. They saw the reporting process as a burden. But through these workshops, we began talking about the reporting process as an important means of building communication, sharing information and strengthening ongoing partnerships with donors. When we talk about longer-term relationships, we are talking about expanding and strengthening a diverse resource base for the future. It is this orientation towards the future of the organization—rather than securing funding for a particular project—that we tried to promote through these workshops.

Within a year of these workshops, several of the groups that had taken part had indeed expanded their funding base. Groups in San Cristóbal, San Luis Potosí, and Tijuana established contact with and received funding for the first time from private foundations in the United States and Canada, as well as from UN agencies. Three years later, in the preparations for the Fourth World Conference on Women in Beijing, the organization staff were able to see that many of the women's groups they had convened for the workshops were still working together. Some, such as those in Oaxaca, had continued to meet primarily to share information. In Tijuana, three of the groups that participated in the workshop had developed collective proposals and were working together to seek funding.

Becoming a catalyst for creating sustainable institutions

Soon after the first workshop series was completed, the Sociedad went through significant upheaval, resulting from the usual growing pains. The time and energy required to deal with internal problems of miscommunication resulted in a temporary halt of the organization's funding and technical assistance programme. In 1995 the organization was restructured and reorganized; some members resigned, some new ones were invited, and the board of directors and the staff both changed considerably and made a strong and successful effort to bring in women from a wide range of disciplines and fields. Board and staff joined in a conscious effort at constituency building, involving outreach to women in the banking world, the corporate world, the media and other fields where alliances with grassroots women's organizations have been few. In this second phase of its existence, the organization is developing new strategies for resource mobilization that go beyond proposal writing and asking for funds from international organizations and individuals. One strategy has been to use a simpler and more provocative name: Semillas ("seeds"). Semillas is redefining the concept of seed money, in line with new strategies for locating and distributing funds.

The fundraising training that the organization provided to Mexican women's groups has positioned it to develop collaborations with foreign donors that increase the flow of funds to Mexico. With one Dutch funding organization for women, for instance, Semillas is developing a relationship that allows the donor to choose to give to a group directly or—where the donor is interested in supporting work in an emerging area but lacks knowledge of specific groups—it gives the funds and Semillas chooses the groups. In another instance, the British government is interested in supporting a group in Mexicali, near the border with the United States. Semillas is providing technical assistance to the group in negotiating the proposal and acts as a point of contact for the group with the British embassy in Mexico City.

In this second phase, demand for support from the organization has increased significantly. In 1996, it expects to receive about 40 qualifying proposals, of which it will only be able to support 15. Maintaining its commitment to generate funds in various innovative ways, Semillas is also acting as a broker. For instance, it convinced the Levi Strauss Company, a major international apparel manufacturer based in California, to give $30,000 to train women working in the *maquiladoras* around Mexico City in non-traditional jobs. In another instance, it assisted a group of women lithographers in securing start-up funds from a Mexican corporation. In many situations, Semillas lends expertise to groups that have requested money from the organization, thereby enabling the groups to secure financing and helping the women's funding effort to build a broader base in the country.

In developing new strategies, Semillas is learning about fundraising techniques that have been successful in North America and adapting these to a local context. A new and exciting effort is a campaign to have wealthy families make a social investment in women by "adopting" a project. This requires broader promotion and outreach than proposal writing and involves the organization in thinking more creatively about inspiring new allies. The women from the mainstream media and corporations who now serve on the organization's board are critical in helping it to achieve this kind of outreach. The organization is using television to reach larger and different segments of the population as well, advertising a phone number that women's organizations can call for help with fundraising and to acquire information on how to apply for Semillas's grants. The organization is also reaching out to painters, musicians and other artists, asking them to hold concerts or sell paintings and pledge a portion of their profits to the fund. When these commitments are organized around a public event—as they were in a public exhibition where well-known painters of Oaxaca donated their works—the organization has the opportunity to obtain wider recognition, generate publicity, and more deliberately influence public opinion and consciousness about its goals.

A second round of workshops

As it builds organizational identity and programmatic flexibility during this second phase, Semillas is once again thinking about its role in building the capacity of women's organizations to generate reliable sources of support for their work. The organization continues to provide technical assistance to groups to improve their proposals, which is really about helping them through a planning process and finding ways to package their ideas. Semillas also continues in its work of encouraging groups to work across different Mexican states in developing collaborative projects and seeking joint funding. One such initiative, bringing together groups from six Mexican states—Jalisco, Michoacán, Guanajuato, Colima, Aguascalientes, San Luis Potosí—resulted in a proposal to the John D. and Catherine T. MacArthur Foundation that gained support for collaborative work on reproductive rights.

In 1995, Semillas received five requests to continue the workshop series and has plans to offer sessions in 1996 in Morelia, Jalisco, Chihuahua and Veracruz. Cristina Zepeda, the current executive director of the organization, believes that the workshops should build on those held in 1992, but incorporate a stronger component oriented towards finding new sources of funding, such as individual women of wealth, local corporate support and mass media campaigns. She commented:

> There continues to be competition between women's groups for money, and Semillas has a role to play in changing attitudes in that regard. Our belief is that, in the women's movement, the more financing we have, the more power we have. The more power we have, the more activities and actions we can undertake.
>
> The challenge is to be able to train a larger number of organizations who become sophisticated in securing funds, so that we address this imbalance of having a few groups that are very well financed—and frequently located in Mexico City—while the majority of women's organizations are struggling. It is more difficult to work with the smaller and poorly financed organizations because they have not "professionalized" their operations in the way that donors like to see. We are committed to helping precisely these organizations, though, and continuing to connect them with more powerful institutions. Our training needs to specifically address the issues of leadership and power in work around money. In a country like Mexico—where questions about class and race are always at the forefront—we have to address the issue of power very directly.
>
> We try to model the behaviour that we think will benefit the entire women's movement in the long run. We are committed to sharing information and providing training to the groups that are most vulnerable and that have the least access. Of the requests that we receive, we may be more inclined to give funds to a good proposal, but we also prioritize providing technical assistance and other forms of support to those whose proposals contain good ideas but reflect a lack of experience. We want to contribute to building a critical mass of groups that have good contacts and that can survive.

Survival of women's organizations is at the core of Semillas's work. While it understands that a key element of its mandate relates to mobilizing new resources for women's organizing, that mandate goes hand in hand with the imperative of building the infrastructure of the women's movement by supporting the growth and strengthening of women's organizations and networks. Many questions remain as it develops its strategies and programmes. Some of the major issues relate to power: How will power dynamics change and be managed if Semillas is successful in securing funds for women from individual donors? What motivates individual donors to give, and is that motivation consistent with the values and principles that Semillas supports? As Semillas grows in its ability to mobilize resources for women, how can it deal straightforwardly with its own decision-making power in relation to grant-making? Other issues relate to the structure of the organization itself and the way it uses the funds it raises. To what extent should Semillas play a role in educating mainstream donors? What level of involvement should the grantees and potential grantees of the organization have in making funding decisions?

In an era of shrinking resources for foreign aid and debates about the roles and responsibilities of the state and governments, it is more critical than ever for women's funds to grow and thrive. The challenges and achievements of organizations such as Semillas offer important lessons that women worldwide can learn from and build on. The interdependence and synergy that is growing between women's funds and the organizations they support provide opportunities to deepen dialogue on many areas of debate—self-sufficiency, power relations, accountability and the future—that the women's movement has grappled with since its inception. ❖

---

1 *Who Benefits, Who Decides? An Agenda for Improving Philanthropy: The Case for Women and Girls*, a Report prepared by the National Council for Research on Women in collaboration with Women and Philanthropy and The National Network of Women's Funds. 1995.

Notes on Contributors

Sonia de Avelar is a political scientist specializing in labour and urban studies. As director of the Feminist Research Centre (CENPROFEM) in São Paulo, she has conducted policy-oriented research on women and labour issues and economic development in Latin America for various UN and other international agencies. She is a member of the Inter-American Development Bank's Permanent Roster of Researchers and Director for Cultural and Scientific Affairs of the Brazilian chapter of the MERCOSUR Women's Forum.

Ana Maria Brasileiro is the Chief of UNIFEM's Political Empowerment Programme. Previously she held the position of Chief of UNIFEM's Latin American and Caribbean Section. Prior to joing UNIFEM, Dr. Brasileiro worked for UNICEF from 1980 to 1992 and also served as the Executive Director of Fundacao Educar in Brazil.

Delaine Martins Costa has been a member of the Women and Public Policy Nucleus of the Brazilian Institute of Municipal Administration (IBAM) since its creation in 1990 and is now the coordinator of that organization. A participant in the Gender, Policy and Planning Course of the Development Planning Unit at University College, London, she has published widely on issues related to gender and organizational development.

Lucero Gonzalez, a founding member of Sociedad Mexicana pro Derechos de la Mujer, currently works on human rights education for GIRE (Grupo de Información en Reproducción Elegida).

Karen Judd is an anthropologist who specializes in women's economic and development issues. She is currently an editorial and communications consultant, working with UNIFEM and other women's and human rights organizations.

Gleisi Heisler Neves is head of the Division of Organization and Management of the Brazilian Institute of Municipal Administration (IBAM). With over 20 years experience in research and technical assistance, especially in the area of local government and urban development, she has participated in several of IBAM's Women and Public Policy Nucleus projects and has authored publications on public policy and management.

Joanne Sandler is an organizational development consultant, trainer and writer who works with women's organizations in the United States and internationally. She consults frequently with UNIFEM.

Meryl James Sebro is a national of Trinidad and Tobago who has worked as a social scientist and gender specialist for national, regional and international agencies in the Caribbean for several years, in the course of which she has helped shape the design of the UNIFEM programme in the Caribbean.

Gina Zabludovsky is a professor of political science at the National Autonomous University of Mexico. She has done extensive research on women in business and management in Mexico, family owned enterprises, and sociological theory. She is currently researching women managers and executives and their participation in interest-group associations.

Women's Leadership in a Changing World
was printed and bound in Mexico by
Corporación Industrial Gráfica, S.A. de C.V.,
Cerro 3 Marías No. 354, Col. Campestre
Churubusco, 04200, Mexico City,
Tel. (5) 544 73 40, Fax (5) 544 72 91

1,000 copies were printed

The edition was supervised by the Mexico
Office of the United Nations Development Fund for Women.